DIGITAL IMPACT

DIGITAL IMPACT

IMPACT

The Human Element of AI-Driven Transformation

STEVE LUCAS

WILEY

Published by John Wiley & Sons, Inc., Hoboken, New Jersey.
Published simultaneously in Canada.

For general information on our other products and services or for technical support, please contact our Customer Care Department within the United States at (800) 762-2974, outside the United States at (317) 572-3993, or fax (317) 572–4002.

Wiley also publishes its books in a variety of electronic formats. Some content that appears in print may not be available in electronic formats. For more information about Wiley products, visit our web site at www.wiley.com.

Library of Congress Control Number: 2025900909

ISBN: 9781394295241 (cloth)
ISBN: 9781394295258 (ePub)
ISBN: 9781394295265 (ePDF)

Cover Image: © Rabbit_1990/Adobe Stock Photos
Cover Design: Wiley

SKY10098763_022425

This book is dedicated to our customers, partners, and the passionate team of innovators at Boomi, who are all working to make an impact with technology, and to my incredible family, whom I treasure.

Contents

Contents

Foreword

By R. "Ray" Wang
Founder, Chairman, and Principal Analyst,
Constellation Research

Almost every leader grapples with a confluence of forces that will transform their organization for better or for worse. Artificial intelligence (AI) is one of those forces. Not only will it impact future business models, but it will also reset winners and losers in every market landscape. So, the question is not whether AI will disrupt – instead, it is, "What will you do with AI to disrupt the market?"

The last great disruption came from the Internet Age. While academics and pundits will claim we have been in some Fourth Industrial Revolution for the purposes of convening world leaders at a very cold venue in January (and they were wrong), AI is truly the next great disruption. Now there are many parallels to previous disruptions. We've tried hard to say mobile was a disruption. Cloud played a key role in changing technology deployments. And digital transformation created new business models. While these statements are all true and these mini-waves were all disruptions, the magnitude of these disruptions really fell back into the Internet Age bucket. Moreover, with the rise of AI, the demarcation between the Internet Age and the Age of AI has become radically apparent in hindsight.

We are at the beginning of this next massive disruption, and, like the Internet Age, the rules will be rewritten. However, the Internet Age was different. The Internet Age ushered in four key attributes – open systems, decentralized control, many winners, and exponentially lower costs. In this Age of AI, we have the exact opposite – closed systems, centralized control, a few winners, and exponentially greater costs. While some of these four attributes will evolve, we will move from chaos to cohesion as the dust settles.

So, success in the Age of AI will require a more precise and disciplined approach. As Steve Lucas highlights in this book, the digital imperative in the Age of AI is here in front of us. Achieving great outcomes with digital transformation requires the ability to master data; use automation to achieve machine scale; and apply AI to augment, accelerate, automate, agentize, and advise our businesses.

AI cannot succeed without a strong data foundation, and businesses must weave AI into the fiber of the entire organization. Organizations will need to rapidly integrate data, seamlessly orchestrate processes, and contextually serve up relevant experiences. This will make the difference between a good business and a great one. With this new Age of AI, we can accomplish great things at machine scale. More importantly, we must also design for human scale.

As you embark on this AI journey, and Steve helps show you the possibilities for your business, I leave you with five questions to ask as you move from proofs of concept to real-world activations:

1. **Where and when do you insert a human?** Most design aesthetics focus on when and where to automate. Determining when human judgment is required will provide a more effective and efficient design point.

2. **Can you operate at machine scale with humans?** Machines are making thousands of decisions per second. Humans may

not be able to catch up. So, how do you harmonize human scale with machine scale?

3. **Do you have enough data to get to precision decisions that your stakeholders will trust?** Achieving precision decisions requires internal and external data sources. For example, 85% accuracy in CX may be okay, but 85% accuracy in finance, someone goes to jail. Worse, are you okay with 85% in health care?

4. **Who do you partner with to create the last mile or last inch of data?** Organizations will have to partner for more and more data across industry value chains to achieve a high level of comfort and trust. Marketplaces for precision data will emerge.

5. **Who do you sue when something goes wrong?** Does the blame lie with the system, the operator, the partner, or another third party? Liability will play a key role in AI deployments.

As you can tell, the winners will apply AI to automate the decision-automation cycle. In fact, projects that deliver a tangible return on transformation investment (RTI)[a] focus on decision automation, not just the technology in AI, but how these new systems move from agents to advisors and answer the key question – how humans and AI will work together.

Decision automation applies business rules, data analysis, workflows, and AI to automate the decision-making process in both operations and strategy. This could be knowing when to make ad buys for a campaign, change pricing for dynamic discounting, send follow-up texts for a future upsell/cross-sell, increase shifts at the factory to meet production demand, adjust invoices and discounts based on interest rates, or determine when to check in on customer satisfaction after a new purchase.

Every organization and leader now has an imperative to reimagine how AI will create better outcomes. The success and failure to harness the forces of disruption rests with your ability to master AI. If you are reading this book, I doubt you will fail.

Through your efforts and understanding, you will achieve digital impact and succeed by delivering a human impact to AI-driven transformation.

Introduction: The Digital Imperative in the Age of AI

We stand at a crossroads where technology isn't just evolving – it's rewriting the rules. This book is your guide to mastering that change.

The phrase "digital transformation" was somewhat born out of the movement. In general, it captures the trend from paper-based systems to truly digital systems. But digital transformation has evolved well beyond that. It has moved from digitizing paper processes to integrating, automating, and connecting systems that empower people to work smarter, not harder.

My personal point of view, after living in the enterprise software world for nearly 30 years, is that the applications involved in digital transformation are somewhat irrelevant. Your company has countless applications. A technology infrastructure is by nature heterogeneous, and all these systems were largely built in a vacuum. Salesforce doesn't talk to SAP, Microsoft doesn't talk to Oracle, etc. This is the nature of software vendors and their strategy to force you to adopt their "stack." But in the end, we all know that no one software company can solve all our needs. Hence, the complex subway map we all stare at when we talk about enterprise architecture.

Regardless of which technology vendor – SAP, Salesforce, Microsoft, Oracle, etc. – may have persuaded you that their system is the way to go, *it doesn't really matter.* At the heart of every technological shift are the people who drive it – your team, your customers, and your leadership.

This book focuses on how connecting and empowering these people through technology leads to true transformation.

As we've moved from paper-based systems to interconnected digital environments, we've arrived at a new frontier: artificial intelligence (AI), the force that is poised to redefine everything. AI isn't just another tool. It's transforming how we connect, innovate, and lead. I will go as far as to say that everything we know about digital technology and the systems powering the world as we know it is going to change thanks to AI. Starting now.

If you blinked, you might have missed the moment when AI made the quantum leap from science fiction into our everyday reality.

When I first encountered AI, it wasn't just a new technology. It was a glimpse into the future. A future where systems not only connect but think and evolve. Upon my first use of ChatGPT (generative AI) in late November 2022, I was enthralled, flabbergasted, and astounded. The conversational chatbot was like nothing I had ever seen. It was as if the words of the late writer Arthur C. Clarke had sprung to life. *Any sufficiently advanced technology is indistinguishable from magic.*[1]

In that blink of an eye, I realized what the developers at OpenAI already knew. Our world had been forever transformed. It was like watching a mind-bending magic trick and trying to understand how it was happening. How was the groundbreaking chatbot doing this? How was it immediately providing answers to anything I asked? How could I make any request, even something as silly as, "Write me a Shakespearean sonnet in the voice of beloved Star Wars character Yoda," and see it just appear? Or, on a more practical level, how did I only describe an application I wanted, and it writes workable code to create it almost instantaneously?

It was a thunderbolt from the blue – much like my first experience using the Internet, listening to digital music, or holding an iPhone in my hand. I knew this would change things.

It was also profoundly humbling. I've spent nearly three decades with leading technology companies at the forefront of innovation, such as Microsoft, SAP, Salesforce, and Adobe. I've been the Chief Executive Officer (CEO) of three software companies. I've witnessed firsthand the transformative power of technology. I thought I was well-connected with trends and dialed into the research around artificial intelligence. Instead, I had been completely blindsided. How could I have not seen this coming?

In that split second, I recognized that all I had ever known about software would change drastically in the coming years. My previous worldview of technology and how it helps businesses operate had been shattered. Now, it would have to be rebuilt because we had suddenly embarked on a great rethinking of technology and how we use it.

Over the short time since OpenAI's announcement and the flurry of other AI advancements that arrived with breathtaking speed, we've all learned about things such as generative pre-trained transformers (GPTs), large language models (LLMs), neural networks, and agents. But understanding how AI works still doesn't spoil the "trick" for me. Instead, I've become even more convinced that our businesses will never be the same.

This is why I believe everything we know about software is going to change.

Unlike magic tricks, the AI revolution is no illusion. It's a fundamental reshaping of everything. It's happening before our eyes, and we all have to move quickly and adapt to this rapidly evolving landscape. We've come a long way from the early days of digital transformation, which were focused on moving apps, and later infrastructure, from on premises to the cloud. Now, everything is going to be pressure-tested by AI.

The digital revolution that began decades ago with the first computer has exploded into an AI-driven future that promises to disrupt every aspect of our lives. We stand at the precipice of a new era, where the lines between human intelligence and artificial intelligence blur and intertwine, where data flows like electricity, and where connectivity is as vital as oxygen.

This all frames one of my main points – that AI's true power lies in its ability to connect disparate systems, transforming fragmented processes into cohesive, intelligent workflows that adapt in real time.

Integration and automation aren't just buzzwords. They're the foundational elements that enable AI to function effectively within your organization, turning fragmented systems into a unified, intelligent enterprise.

Of course, you're probably wondering about the same question I did: "How can AI change what businesses do?" I think it's clear for the 17 year old who wants help with their homework. But what about the software that powers organizations? What about sales? What about business processes?

As CEO of an integration and automation software company, I constantly ask: "How will this radical shift in capability – where applications can now reason – reshape organizations, their systems, and processes?" This shift demands that the C-suite rethink how their businesses operate from end to end.

The possibilities for infusing AI into processes are endless. It could radically transform health care, improve education, help address climate change, and, yes, make our businesses more efficient and our customers happier. At the same time, the challenge for each of us is navigating the profound changes that come with AI and leveraging the technology to our best advantage.

This shift into the AI era also highlights a fundamental, existential problem that every organization must urgently confront. We explore that problem in this book.

Beneath the gleaming surface of this digital utopia lies a chaotic underbelly within our businesses – a tangled web of fragmented systems, isolated data silos, and disconnected processes.

This lack of cohesion was already the hidden crisis of our time. But now, it's further exacerbated by the advent of GPTs, LLMs, agents, and the coming wave of AI-fueled disruption. Digital fragmentation threatens to derail the AI revolution for your business before it truly begins. If we don't address the chaos of disconnected systems now, the AI revolution could slip through our fingers before we even begin to harness its power.

The stakes have never been higher. Addressing digital fragmentation is no longer optional – it's imperative. Otherwise, the promise of AI will remain out of reach. Furthermore, we all like to think we live in a world where everything is connected. But is it connected properly? When it's not, nothing works. As you will see, this is especially the case with AI.

Connected Technology and Its Impact on My Life

Technology can do amazing things to change the world. I'm a living, breathing example of how it can have a transformative impact on people. My journey in technology isn't just professional. It's deeply personal.

In my mid-20s, I was diagnosed with Type 1 diabetes. In this life-threatening condition, the pancreas stops producing insulin, a vital hormone that regulates the glucose in your blood. Initially, I was left reeling and, at the risk of sounding overly dramatic, believed that the future I had envisioned for myself was over. But nothing could have been further from the truth. Over time, I've come to believe that diabetes has made me a better, more empathetic person. I've lived a rich life *because* of diabetes, not *despite* it.

But that doesn't mean that managing diabetes has been easy, as any of the approximately 1.3 million adults in the United States alone who are living with the condition can tell you.[2] During the first 15 years of coping with it, I estimate that I probably administered about 50,000 injections of insulin, assuming 8–10 doses a day. It's like you're a scientist, constantly monitoring a chemistry experiment inside your body, 24/7/365. It's notoriously challenging to match the correct amount of insulin with your food intake, and very bad things can happen if you take too much or too little.

Here's where technology enters the picture, ultimately leading to the reason why I wrote this book. Over the years, medical technology innovation has made it easier for people with diabetes to thrive, not just survive. Preloaded insulin pens were introduced to replace syringes. Then came pumps and continuous glucose monitoring sensors. Today, I wear a pump on one side of my abdomen with a several-day insulin supply and a glucose monitor that measures my blood sugar level on the other side.

The sensor and the pump talk to each other via an algorithm that acts as one's natural endocrine system would. It connects the two devices and automatically administers the correct dosage of insulin. It's like I have a working pancreas again. Only I wear mine on the outside of my body. (I think I officially qualify as a cyborg, which is pretty cool.) This interactive system features:

- **Technology:** Remarkable advancements in ubiquitous computing, nanoscience, and wearable medical devices.
- **Integration:** The ability to connect two disparate technologies to communicate about my body chemistry in real time.
- **Automation:** The automating of insulin delivery at the appropriate dosage.

This miracle of connected technologies isn't just about convenience. It's a life-changing innovation that allows me, and people like me, to live more fully and focus on what matters most.

My health history gives me a unique appreciation of the power of connected technology. But this personal experience mirrors the journey many businesses are on today. Just as my health management evolved from manual injections to an automated and connected system, organizations are grappling with the need to move from fragmented, siloed operations into seamlessly integrated, AI-enhanced processes.

Almost every business purchased and implemented each of its systems individually, to solve an array of specific business needs. Think of all the digital systems you rely on today within your operations: enterprise resource planning (ERP), customer relationship management (CRM), supply chain management (SCM), human resource management (HRM), marketing automation, cloud-based applications, data warehouses and lakes, edge systems, public and private clouds, etc. The list seems endless – and it's growing longer every day. That's why our digital architectures are a mess.

Individually, those foundational systems play pivotal roles in business, ensuring that specific functions run smoothly. But company-wide efficiency occurs only when they're connected and genuinely work together. Orchestrating those systems and processes through connectivity has the capability of changing the trajectory of your business. The improbable becomes possible if systems operate as one, workflows are seamless, and data is readily available to those who need it.

You probably know from hard-earned experience that this nirvana of connectivity is difficult to achieve. But perhaps what you don't yet realize is that it's even more essential in the age of AI. Businesses with disconnected systems will not survive the coming changes. You can have the shiniest, fanciest AI model at the heart of your business. But AI won't understand your business if your systems aren't integrated, and processes aren't automated. The technology won't have the context that comes with understanding your CRM system, sales and marketing motion, invoice process-ing, ticket handling, and everything else. It won't know because it won't have access to your trusted, proprietary data. AI won't have the intelligence to make the right decisions for your business and deliver the best outcomes.

This isn't much different from how a human brain won't function properly when the biological neural pathways are dis-connected or disrupted. The digital neural networks of AI can't perform their best without clear pathways providing the right information.

When I was growing up, my grandfather would tell me that if you can't say something quickly, you can't say it at all. It was great advice then and now. So, let me be clear: For businesses to succeed in the age of AI, they must be relentlessly focused on integrating and automating their systems. It's the only way to drive what we refer to many times throughout this book as *AI-fueled* digital transformation. Or, said more succinctly, AI-field change.

Why This Book? Why Now?

I believe we're at a critical juncture. The promises of digital transformation have often fallen short, leaving many businesses disillusioned and struggling with increased complexity rather than enhanced efficiency. Trust me, I've lived through the challenges of rapid digital advancement and seen the many pitfalls. Now, as we stand on the brink of widespread AI adoption, it's crucial that we learn from these past experiences and build a solid foundation for the future.

Why Should You Consider My Perspective?

Today, I lead Boomi, the world's largest independent, AI-driven integration and automation company.[3] The roots of the company's name tell the Boomi story. It derives from the Hindi word *Bhumi*, which loosely translates to "of the earth." Boomi's founders believed our technology is foundational to business success because everything works better when systems, processes, and people are connected.

But I'm not here to pitch a product. I don't like to be sold on something, and I doubt you do. No one wants to be marketed to, either. (That's one of the first lines I wrote in a previous book about the engagement economy, *Engage to Win*.[4]) But we all want the kind of advice and guidance that helps us make better decisions, solve problems, and keep our businesses heading in the right direction.

Digital Impact is your guide through this new labyrinth, a beacon of clarity in the fog of technological hype, and it will show you how to make AI practical within your business. I've structured the book to take you on a journey – one I'm experiencing right along with you. Think of me as your sherpa as we climb to the mountaintop together. We start at base camp by examining the current state of digital fragmentation and its impact on businesses. Then, we begin our ascent with the key elements necessary for creating a truly connected, AI-ready organization: integration, data management, automation, application programming interface (API) management, and agent management.

The thread woven throughout the book's fabric is the theme that every business needs to interconnect the critical business objects of applications, data, APIs, and now AI agents. The successful cohesion of these essential elements, if you will, is at the core of navigating digital transformation. Following this thread leads us to explore several fundamental concepts that will help your business be more successful today and better prepared for whatever the AI future brings.

- **The Integration Imperative:** We address how integration is the bedrock of digital success. It's an invisible force that turns disparate technologies into a symphony of productivity. Connectivity can be a superpower for your business.

- **Data: The New Oil or the New Sand?** We challenge conventional wisdom about data and explain why more isn't necessarily better. We discuss how you can transform your data from a burden into a strategic asset that fuels AI and drives decision-making.

- **The Automation Revolution:** We examine how intelligent automation creates efficiencies, improves productivity, and frees human potential and creativity.

- **How APIs Are the Hidden Backbone of the Digital World:** We unveil the crucial role of APIs as the digital connective tissue that creates a flexible, scalable digital ecosystem ready for the AI age.

- **The Rise of the Machines (That Work for Us):** We examine the emergence of AI agents – not as science fiction but as practical tools that already are reengineering how businesses operate.

- **The Human Element:** Throughout this journey, we never lose sight of the most critical factor – how these technologies impact people.

I want to pause on the last bullet point because it holds special meaning for me. At this inflection point, there's a deep concern that these technological advances, as wondrous as they potentially are, will also de-emphasize people and their roles within organizations.

AI represents a tectonic shift in how our businesses will operate. But the problem is that with any digital transformation, we too often focus on the technology itself and not how it affects people. This is a mistake. My goal is to explain how real digital transformation has to be human-centric in order to be successful. AI and automation are powerful, but their success hinges on one thing: the people who use them. Without a human-centric approach, even the most advanced technology will fail

As humans, the way we connect is through stories. So, I'm so proud to have the opportunity to share some amazing stories of how organizations such as Australian Red Cross, Tony's Chocolonely, and the Credit Union of Colorado are leveraging the connectivity of technology in innovative ways to make a real difference in people's lives. You'll see how each one never loses sight of the human impact of technology as part of their mission. They all lead with empathy, sincerely desire to help people, and always seek ways to grow their impact. These stories aren't just inspiring; they're proof that we can change the world when we get digital transformation right.

You also won't hear just from me as we venture through these pages. That would be boring, and I'm not sure I want to listen to myself for that long. I've sought out true industry titans, visionary technology leaders, and AI pioneers to share their wisdom. Their insights, combined with real-world case studies, will ground our exploration in practical, actionable strategies.

When speaking publicly, I often talk about how much I love the transformative power of technology. (Nerdy but true!) I'm a technologist who believes IT departments are the unsung heroes of modern business. In that spirit, I want readers familiar with the day-to-day challenges around digital fragmentation to gain valuable knowledge about the efficiencies possible with a connected architecture. However, as a CEO, I see everything through a business lens and understand there has to be clear value for any technology initiative.

My goal is to strike a balance for everyone, both technical and nontechnical, and provide a roadmap for success in the AI-driven future. Whether you're a CEO charting your company's digital strategy, a CIO grappling with technological complexity, or a business leader just trying to make sense of the AI revolution, *Digital Impact* offers a clear path forward.

No book about AI can be definitive because we're so early in the game. Right now, we still don't know what we don't know. But a book can be directional. This one is designed to provide guidance and support as you harness AI's potential to propel your organization into a future of unprecedented productivity and innovation. More than anything, I hope it makes you think.

We've reached a nexus in the world of enterprise software. The future isn't just coming – it's already here. It's more complex, more interconnected, and filled with more potential than we ever imagined. It's a little scary too. But I firmly believe every business can succeed when it turns digital fragmentation into digital cohesion.

When you can focus on creating systems that don't just process data but generate insights and drive action, something amazing happens: magic.

As you dive into the chapters ahead, keep in mind that the choices you make today about integrating and automating your systems will define the future of your business. You have the power to take control, embrace change, and lead your organization into a future where digital cohesion creates the real magic.

Chapter 1

From Chaos to Cohesion: Mastering AI-Driven Transformation

What we discuss in this chapter:

- The real reason why digital transformation initiatives often fail.
- How your success with AI will depend on the degree of connectivity within your digital architecture.
- How Australian Red Cross unified a complex digital ecosystem with a single layer of connectivity to better help people in need.

"If Red Cross couldn't respond to disasters, who would?"

On the evening of March 12, 2022, the eyes of a nation were on the IT team at Australian Red Cross.[5]

Actually, Australians were fixated on the country's three national television networks. They had banded together to broadcast a star-studded telethon called "Australia Unites" to raise desperately needed disaster relief funds after historic flooding in Queensland and New South Wales.

Viewers watched celebrities such as Hugh Jackman, Nicole Kidman, Keith Urban, and Cate Blanchett urge fellow Australians to give what they could to help people who, in some cases, had lost everything. Behind the scenes, Australian Red Cross' IT team was under tremendous pressure to ensure its digital operations withstood an unprecedented surge in donations.

"It was like a duck swimming on a pond," said Chief Information Officer Brett Wilson. "It might have looked like we were cruising along nicely. But beneath the water, our little legs were moving a million miles an hour. We know how to react quickly at Red Cross. But nothing had ever been done before at this scale, and expectations were significant that the technology needed to provide a flawless experience."

The back-office systems functioned brilliantly. Australian Red Cross' website, which typically has about 300 unique visitors at any given time, handled an average of 10,000 visitors – processing 11 donations per second over five-plus hours without a hitch. The event was a smashing success, ultimately raising $32 million – all directly going to help people.[6]

This was a remarkable achievement, and not just because the event came together in just five days. Australian Red Cross was in the early stages of a digital transformation initiative to radically overhaul its aging architecture. The organization still relied on antiquated technologies that limited its operations even under normal circumstances.

Australian Red Cross' team had one significant advantage: an AI-driven integration and automation platform from Boomi.

This platform enabled the IT staff to scale up several legacy systems on short notice. For example, the organization's customer relationship management (CRM) system, without the integration and automation platform, could normally only execute about 30 transactions every 10 minutes. The Boomi Enterprise Platform's capabilities supercharged that speed, enabling Australian Red Cross to process 300,000 donations in 24 hours. This meant the not-for-profit could unlock funds faster to support the community.

"Even with all those legacy systems, we had that modern platform sitting in the middle, connecting everything," Wilson added. "It was a key piece of technology that made the night a success because we would not have been able to handle that volume without it."

Australian Red Cross has a simple yet profound mission: assisting people. Approximately 1,600 staff, 8,000 members, and 25,000 volunteers deliver humanitarian and community services. The organization operates retail stores and oversees initiatives like the Young Parents Program, which supports mothers and children, assists immigrants, and helps First Nations people. When disasters strike, Australian Red Cross runs toward danger, not away.

Two years before those epic floods, the organization was instrumental in helping Australians rebuild their lives following terrible bushfires. At the time, Wilson was in corporate IT, where he had focused on simplifying complex technology environments in industries that included construction, manufacturing, and finance. When his aunt nearly lost her home in the fires that devastated her community, Wilson organized an effort to donate supplies and campers as temporary housing for those who had lost their homes. Soon afterward, Wilson joined Red Cross because he saw an opportunity to make a more significant impact.

"Australian Red Cross does so many amazing things," Wilson said. "But when our people are in the field, they need the information to make decisions and act on them quickly. Time is always of the essence. Older, archaic systems are quite challenging. They add to the time it takes to help someone. If we have an emergency and then have to figure out how to access information, it slows things down."

One notable example of digital chaos was that 89% of the 200-plus applications at Australian Red Cross consisted of "shadow IT" – deployed without the technical team's knowledge or oversight. The result was siloed data, poor visibility into basic operations, increased security risks, and ultimately fragmented customer experiences.

The IT team spent about 18 months creating a new digital spine by implementing seven core technologies, including CRM, HR, marketing automation, an enterprise data platform, finance, and risk assessment systems. The objective was to create a single view of staff, volunteers, and donors with trusted data. That would increase organizational speed, improve efficiency, and make Red Cross better financial stewards.

Australian Red Cross used the Boomi platform to stitch everything together and deliver on its mission. The platform replaced a complex mix of point-to-point integrations with a single connectivity layer. It helped the team reduce the number of applications and costs in the organization's tech stack, integrate systems more quickly, automate processes, and create a unified architecture with a complete view of operations.

"The platform enables Australian Red Cross to connect a lot more systems and platforms, a lot easier and simpler," Wilson said. "The less money we spend on the back office, the more we can provide help and support during a disaster or in a community program. It always comes down to the fact that we have a finite amount of money, and how do we use it most effectively? The platform helps us do that."

For instance, automating a cash assistance program for migrants eliminated 11 of 12 manual processes, saving an estimated 451 days of manual effort each year. And, as Australian Red Cross' transformation journey continues, Wilson said they're excited about the platform's AI functionality for using natural language requests to integrate systems. By eliminating the technical skills required for connecting systems, Australian Red Cross speeds up development time, uses IT resources more effectively, and saves money.

Other AI-related projects that will depend on seamless connectivity include creating more personalized donor experiences to increase fundraising, automating processes with third-party vendors to ensure no humans encounter personally identifiable information, and developing a "smart bot" to speed operations. If a staff member in the field needs information quickly, an AI assistant support bot can immediately provide access. Wilson said the conservative estimate is that over three years, it will resolve around 20,000 calls and eliminate 1.3 million hours of wait time.

"Sometimes terms like AI and transformation are overused," Wilson added. "But they really mean something to us. They're about finding ways to help people faster and ensuring more money goes into the community to do great things. If Red Cross couldn't respond to disasters, who would?"

Key Points

- **Goal:** Improve the organization's speed and efficiency so more money goes directly toward services that help people in need.

- **Human Impact:** Integration and automation play a significant role in transforming an outdated infrastructure, decommissioning about 10% of their applications, deploying seven foundational systems, providing a unified view of operations, and preparing the organization to use AI, which makes providing services more efficient.

- **Lessons Learned:** "I think anything's possible when you have a great team, and you've made sure you have great support around you. When that happens, you can achieve some amazing things. Everyone rallied together to make the telethon successful. That attitude has carried forward in our digital transformation." – *Brett Wilson, Chief Information Officer, Australian Red Cross*

The Power of Connection

Australian Red Cross' journey is a metaphor for what we're addressing in this chapter – how we must prepare to handle challenges, even potential disasters. In this case, Australian Red Cross was prepared and saved lives. Their success during this critical event wasn't just about technology – it was about connection. Connecting systems, people, and data seamlessly made this response possible.

I've stood next to Brett on stage as he tells this digital transformation story, and when you hear him, you get goosebumps. The audience hangs on every word. Everyone can relate to their success in radically simplifying a complex digital architecture. But they also understand that it's about something more: connecting people. Moving forward, digital transformation is about people and connecting everything.

On this topic, it's worth stating I believe in universal truths. There are fundamental concepts in life we can generally agree upon. One is the power of connection. The world is better when we communicate, understand different perspectives, and look out for one another. Connection is the thread that holds humanity together.

This deep-rooted need for connection has been with us since the dawn of humankind. Our earliest Stone Age ancestors exchanged ideas and imparted knowledge by scratching out drawings on cave walls. As the centuries passed, spoken and written language evolved. Then came the printing press, telegraph, telephone, radio, television, computers, and the Internet. Even as the methods of communication have changed and grown, the innate need to connect hasn't. There's not much difference between our ancestors sitting around a campfire and today's virtual social media campfire.

A wealth of research indicates that people with strong social connections are happier. Studies also have shown that people who feel isolated have shorter lifespans and that, as a risk factor, isolation carries a risk of mortality like that of other harmful activities such as smoking.[7] It's almost as if connectivity is the secret to maintaining better, healthier, and more meaningful lives.

However, the negative impact of human disconnection within businesses is profound. It's not just that problems arise when people within organizations don't communicate. Everything slows down when systems, applications, and databases don't talk with one another. Resources get wasted. Customers are unhappy. This is a sad reality for many businesses today.

So, here's another truth I'm hoping to help make universal. Like people, technology systems are better when connected. Incredible things are possible when applications, data, and devices are integrated, and processes are automated. Connectivity helps organizations collaborate more efficiently, gain real-time access to their data for better decision-making, and move faster than the competition. As a (big!) bonus, it also enables people to reach their full potential. The whole becomes greater than the sum of its parts.

But integrating technologies within an organization's complicated digital architecture has never been more challenging. I'm offering this simplified graphic not to be instructional but rather to point out the irony of what we deem "acceptable" in our modern era (Figure 1.1).

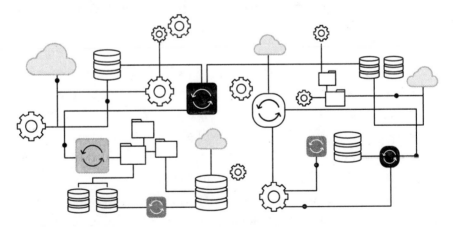

Figure 1.1 Typical digital architecture integration.

From Chaos to Cohesion: Mastering AI-Driven Transformation

It's oddly comforting, right? We somehow look at this and go, "Oh yeah, that's *my* company." The tacit notion is that all our organizations are like this and that the ensuing chaos – lack of integration and connection – somehow bonds us.

The most common reason I hear for any technology project failing is the lack of connectivity. Businesses today are suffering from this notion of digital fragmentation. This will worsen exponentially as we plunge headfirst into this shift of digital eras – the rise of artificial intelligence. And it's about to get even more complicated. As AI enters the chat, so to speak, we require a new way of thinking about how our organizations must be connected, reduce complexity, and find ways to get the most from a disruptive technology that is changing everything.

The Dark Side of Digital Transformation

As I mentioned in the introduction, software companies don't talk to each other. It's worth asking how we got to a point where our most critical systems don't interact well. The answer is, mainly through good intentions and unintended consequences.

To unpack these unintended consequences, just for fun, I asked a child of the digital transformation era – ChatGPT – to define the term as well. It responded: *Digital transformation is the process of utilizing digital technologies to fundamentally change business operations, customer experiences, and value delivery. It's about integrating digital technology into all areas of a business, leading to significant improvements in efficiency, value, and innovation. This transformation reshapes how organizations engage with their customers, streamline processes, and compete in the digital age.*

It's not that far off from what I asserted in the introduction.

Digital transformation might be an abstract concept, but it's another way to describe innovation that helps humans progress.

Once upon a time, innovation was building a better ship to cut a week off your trip across the Atlantic Ocean. Today, innovation can involve countless people – using technology to build code, write systems, and maintain infrastructure within our businesses.

But like beauty, digital transformation is also in the eye of the beholder. It means different things to different organizations depending on where they stand on the technology spectrum. But rest assured, every company is on some kind of digital journey.

If there was a catalyst for modernization in our time, it happened when the world went into lockdown during the global pandemic. Necessity was the mother of invention as every organization suddenly had to pivot to provide remote access to its goods and services. Many did heroic work by moving quickly to offer virtual experiences for shopping, medical appointments, education, and more during that everything-from-home period.

The pandemic got the attention of businesses that hadn't already been thinking digitally. It exposed the widespread lack of digital preparation, and organizations frantically rushed to catch up. In April 2020, Microsoft CEO Satya Nadella famously said the company had "seen two years' worth of digital transformation in two months" as cloud adoption exploded.[8] With the best intentions, businesses loaded up innovative cloud applications and services like kids in a candy store. The goal was to become more agile and provide the "easy button" experiences customers demanded.

Then came the unintended consequences.

Those systems created digital silos, walled gardens obscuring essential data, application sprawl, and technology complexity. Disconnected architecture became the norm. The newer, cloud-based systems had difficulty communicating with one another, and with the critical legacy systems still humming along in data centers. Applications and data sources were everywhere. Connecting and synchronizing them became a monumental challenge. Here are numbers that show the scope of this digital fragmentation:

- One study determined that larger organizations (2,000 or more employees) deployed an average of 231 applications in 2024 – an increase of 10% from the previous year.[9]

- Dwarfing that data point was another recent survey that found organizations, on average, use 342 SaaS applications. It also determined that the typical business department relies on about 73 apps.[10]

- Yet another study revealed that 79% of organizations have more than 100 different data sources, and 30% use more than 1,000 sources.[11]

These findings likely underestimate the scope of the problem. As applications have become easier to purchase, it's increasingly common for business units to avoid the delays associated with over-worked and understaffed technical teams. They just implement what we often refer to as "shadow IT." They deploy apps independently, often without the technical teams knowing what's embedded within the company architecture. It's not exactly going rogue, but that lack of oversight can introduce a multitude of risks in the form of security gaps, duplication of systems, inaccessibility, and other negative repercussions for the business.

Simple mathematics dictates the growth in complexity and fragmentation. We can lean on one of those statistics above – that an "average" enterprise organization has more than 342 cloud/SaaS applications. Let's be incredibly conservative and say that each needed to share just 100 data elements for things like order processing, analytics, etc. Then we're talking 34,200 data elements your average organization needs to integrate. What if each of those 100 elements were connected with just two other elements? That's 68,400 connections on top of the elements that must be managed.

Suppose one customer record requires data from three applications, and each application shares 100 data elements. In this case, 300 data elements must be managed and correctly aligned for a single complete customer view. You can do the math. But see how it gets very big, very quickly?

Digital fragmentation isn't easily wrangled, and this explosive growth of applications continues unabated. Meanwhile, attitudes toward digital transformation have noticeably shifted.

Transformation Became Chaos

There's a growing sense of skepticism about digital transformation, if not outright frustration and disillusionment. Businesses have grown more concerned about the vast amounts of expensive technical debt mounting in their operations. They're also paying closer attention to whether lofty promises are being kept. (Spoiler alert: They aren't.)

The Harvard Business Review wrote: "Business leaders, shareholders, and board members have increasingly been saying the same thing – albeit using different words – when it comes to their company's digital and AI transformations. While 89% of large companies globally have a digital and AI transformation underway, they have only captured 31% of the expected revenue lift and 25% of expected cost savings from the effort."[12] McKinsey & Company discovered something similar, concluding: "Most organizations achieve less than one-third of the impact they expected from recent digital investments."[13]

In hindsight, nobody should be surprised that businesses see a poor return on massive investments. The millions spent on innovative, cloud-based applications and systems carried an unexpected price tag. They created Frankenstein-like architectures that added ridiculous amounts of complexity to their operations.

Here's a typical example. Let's say your organization decides to deploy Salesforce as the CRM – a critical system of record for any business. You need to connect that to maybe a dozen other applications and databases. If you just assume that Salesforce has native connectivity for all those different systems, you would probably be wrong. And if it does, it's only the bare minimum and likely won't meet your requirements. That's because interoperability with a host of disparate systems isn't part of Salesforce's primary functionality. Now, multiply that scenario by the other 340-plus applications within a typical enterprise, all of which must be connected to make information easily accessible.

The problem scales quickly. Organizations become fragmented. As each system is typically designed for a particular domain or line of business, it's natural for any connector or integration to be built with the same use case mindset. That spawns even more issues, as only one end of the connection is optimal. It doesn't matter where you are on your digital transformation journey: These digital issues are inevitable, and they will impact you.

Not only is digital fragmentation real, but it also becomes weightier over time. That's why your digital architecture today likely resembles a metropolitan subway map (Figure 1.2). It's also just as confusing. You're trying to connect these massive numbers of systems and information sources so that you can move data, like how subways transport citizens around a city.

No wonder chief information officers, the keepers of our digital ecosystems, have the most challenging job in business today. They're just trying to hold it all together in a world where they no longer have complete control of the company tech stack. Or that chief financial officers (CFO), who control the purse strings for our enterprises, have watched through gritted teeth as technology budgets soared

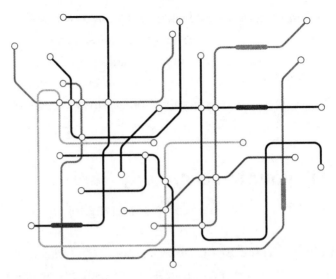

Figure 1.2 Digital architecture map.

only to return paltry results. The tech stack has become a money pit. For instance, a 2024 survey conducted by Forrester Consulting of 420 IT decision-makers found that 72% said their company had exceeded its cloud budget in that fiscal year. The report also noted that public cloud spending should reach more than $1 trillion globally by 2026.[14]

Because I'm mainly focusing on fragmentation in the cloud here, I'm glossing over the fact that most organizations still have significant on-premises tech debt. The good old mainframe computer isn't going away any time soon.

There's a word to describe this costly, complex state of affairs: chaos.

The result is an uncomfortable truth. Despite best efforts, most businesses have consistently failed to achieve their digital transformation aspirations. We still have the same fundamental problems we did when systems resided exclusively in on-premises environments. Can these things talk to each other? Not so much. Can we move data to where it's needed? Not really. The same challenges persist. They endure. Complexity has overwhelmed the enterprise.

From Chaos to Cohesion: Mastering AI-Driven Transformation

But these problems *are* solvable. In fact, a new sense of urgency is forcing every organization to finally address these issues. If businesses can overcome the fundamental challenge of connectivity that has long thwarted their digital transformation ambitions, they will also set the stage for success in the AI era, or they will be left behind. It's that simple.

The AI Revolution Is Already Here

Let's consider the evolution of computer technology:

- **The Mainframe Era (1960s–1970s):** Centralized computing systems introduce data processing and storage at scale.

- **The PC and Client/Server Era (1980s–1990s):** The power of computing reaches the masses with the development of microprocessors.

- **The Internet Era (1990s–2000s):** Global connectivity enables unprecedented information exchange with the rise of the web, email, and ecommerce.

- **The Mobile Era (2000s):** Apple's iPhone, released on June 29, 2007, forever changes how we think of mobile devices and puts connection in the palms of our hands.

- **The Cloud Era (2010s to present):** The untethering of computing resources from traditional data centers leads to a pivot toward cloud data services and SaaS applications, which enable scalability and flexibility.

Irrespective of where you entered the technology world – I started in the PC and client/server era of the 1990s – all these inventions have driven massive, worldwide change. What's beyond question is that innovation cycles have become more compressed. The pace of change has never been more relentless. We're all spinning the hamster wheel faster just to keep up.

Now comes the convergence of all the digital technologies that came before this moment with the creation of perhaps the greatest force for connection we've ever seen:

- **The Artificial Intelligence Era (2022 to present):** On November 30, 2022, OpenAI launched a conversational chatbot powered by a large language model that creates human-like text responses to questions. This resulted in a global awakening: more and more people began to realize the potential – and the perils – of artificial intelligence.

Researchers in this field would argue AI has been around for 50-plus years, and they'd be right. Machine learning has been progressing steadily for decades. However – and that's a BIG however – what distinguishes the AI era from its predecessors is not merely the technology itself, but how it's interwoven into every facet of daily life and work. AI broke out of research labs and theoretical discussions. Now, it's actively reshaping industries, from healthcare diagnostics to autonomous driving to personalized education.

The leap from academic curiosity to global utility underscores the unique trajectory of AI's evolution. Unlike earlier eras, where advancements were often siloed within specific sectors or required specialized knowledge to harness their potential, AI's democratization has made it accessible to a broader audience. Anyone with access to an Internet connection now has a ticket to ride.

Chatbots demonstrate how AI can be as user-friendly as it is powerful, inviting innovation on a scale previously unimaginable. Within a few short days of its release, ChatGPT became a household name and reached 100 million users in just two months. Two short years later, it has become apparent that generative artificial intelligence and autonomous solutions like ChatGPT and others are the vanguard for a technology that will profoundly impact our lives in ways we still can't fully comprehend.

We're experiencing a remarkable digital era shift that will impact every aspect of human existence and radically transform business – and sooner than we think. Ignoring the potential of AI is like continuing to use a slide rule even after the introduction of calculators. And speaking of historical examples, I don't think it's an overstatement to say that the emergence of AI-infused intelligence is like the breakthrough of the antibiotic penicillin; it eclipsed the collective knowledge of the world's best medical minds on how to treat infections.

Still, I do understand why you might be more than a little cynical about AI hype. While some use cases involving deep pattern recognition, code generation, and content summarization were immediately apparent, other examples of practical business value have been slower to reveal themselves. There are also legitimate concerns regarding AI's accuracy, security, privacy, and ethical implications. Nevertheless, this is a profound moment.

The last time something like this happened was when Apple CEO Steve Jobs walked on stage to reveal the iPhone. At that moment, nobody envisioned how this device would completely alter our ability to connect. You couldn't have imagined how tapping something on a phone touchscreen could result in a stranger bringing you a burrito. Or that another stranger would deliver groceries to your home while you stood in line at a coffee shop. Or that you would feel safe getting into yet another stranger's car so they could take you to a doctor's appointment. Back then, it was an ill-advised activity. Today, it's called ridesharing. But now, all of these, and so many more previously unimaginable possibilities, are entirely commonplace.

A similar implausible-to-routine progression is well underway with AI. The essential question is how this convergence of digital transformation and AI will impact our businesses and our lives.

Welcome to the AI Era

If you're waiting for the AI economy to arrive, you missed the launch. It's already here. There's a reason why the world's most valuable technology companies are heavily involved with AI. In 2024 alone, Microsoft, Google, and Meta all confirmed they would spend billions on new data centers for AI.[15] In the larger business community, Goldman Sachs estimated $200 billion globally would be invested in AI by 2025 as projects go from pilots to scale.[16] One investment that blows my mind is how Microsoft and OpenAI are planning to spend as much as $100 billion over five years on a data center project that includes an AI supercomputer.[17] Some analysts estimate $1 trillion could be spent on data centers and energy expenses in the AI boom.[18]

The magnitude of investment is beyond crazy and will reverberate throughout our businesses. It will bring vast disruption and fuel positive transformation at unprecedented speed and scale. Every company, big or small, regardless of industry, is under enormous pressure to implement AI models to improve customer support, supply chain management, software development, predictive analytics, risk management, fraud detection, human resources, and so much more. The impact will reach every aspect of our business operations.

A McKinsey & Company study determined that the number one initiative for CEOs in 2024 was finding how to make AI use cases a reality. The consulting firm wrote: "But while innovators dominate headlines, it's scalers that dominate markets. CEOs need to figure out three things, posthaste: which parts of the business can benefit, how to scale from one application to many, and how the new tools will reshape their industry."[19]

A 2024 PwC survey of more than 4,700 CEOs put that idea in more stark terms. It found that 45% were not confident that their businesses would survive more than a decade on their current path

From Chaos to Cohesion: Mastering AI-Driven Transformation

if they didn't adjust to fast-moving changes that include AI.[20] Leaders know a tsunami is approaching and will leave their companies underwater if they don't figure out how to deploy this business-altering technology.

That's why I believe that if 2024 was the year of AI adoption, then 2025 is the year of AI explosion.

Hello, AI Big Bang!

The cosmic Big Bang created galaxies, stars, planets, and everything we observe in the universe today. Something similar is happening with AI – creating something new and wonderful. It's like nothing I've ever seen in my nearly 30-year career in business, and it's truly transformative. The universe of business opportunities is expanding exponentially.

Right now, "AI" means different things to different people – everything from ChatGPT to fears of Skynet taking over.[21] Sometimes, I get asked to speak to C-level peers about AI developments. At one session with about 200 top leaders, I explained they all needed to get their arms around one game-changing reality: AI agents. These are pieces of software that can mimic human activity. AI agents are programmed to act independently (without direct human intervention) to execute actions, accomplish routine tasks, and automate basic business decision-making.

Think about your typical day. Many of the emails you receive are likely AI-generated. If you scroll through TikTok or Instagram, you'll see AI's influence in the choice of videos suggested to you. Any news you might want to read, food you might want to eat, and things you want to purchase? AI's digital fingerprints are there. And don't get me started on the ads you see on every website, many of which seem to be following you around the Internet. Even when you're relaxing and want to binge-watch a show on Netflix, AI is there, serving up recommendations based on your viewing habits.

AI already influences your life to varying degrees hundreds of times each day. But get ready for something even more significant: the agents are coming.

Common AI models, such as the various iterations of ChatGPT, perform functions when a human triggers them. You ask, and they respond. ("Write me a Yoda-style Shakespearean sonnet.") But autonomous and semi-autonomous agents are next-level AI because they're not mere chatterboxes. They can use software apps and tools, schedule meetings, send emails, analyze data, and more.

We've been ceding ground to forms of AI for at least a decade. But soon, these agents will embed AI even more deeply in our lives.

The first generation of agents is impacting customer success, finance, HR, and more as they help humans work more efficiently. This is just the start. Two years from now, agents will be ubiquitous in our businesses. We'll have agents for everything. Think of them as friendly, valuable minions. I envision organizations deploying small armies of these agents. It will reach the scale where agents will have their own agents to help them accomplish tasks.

The simplest example I can think of is the expense report. Today, managers must approve expenses because we require a human in the loop to interpret and apply company policies. However, within the next 24 months, human approval of expense reports will be a thing of the past. Agents will do it instead.

This is how agents will reinvent how we live and work. We're at the dawn of "The Agent Economy" in the same way the iPhone led to "The App Economy." This is our brave new world, where we'll watch the gap between AI potential and AI value quickly disappear. Right now, it might still be the stuff of science fiction, but soon, we'll have access to a personal AI agent that knows us and helps with daily, mundane tasks – both in and out of work.

A digital era shift is happening. We're witnessing a democratization of hyper-advanced technology, and innovation is happening at

From Chaos to Cohesion: Mastering AI-Driven Transformation

an unprecedented scale. The speed of AI advances makes weeks feel like an eternity. It's hard not to think we only know a fraction of what we need to make sense of AI. But we understand that the consequences are severe if we don't adapt.

Where Do We Go from Here?

It all comes back to connectivity. Integration and automation are the keys to eliminating digital fragmentation and preparing your business for AI.

Becoming AI-Ready

Be highly suspicious if anyone tells you they have AI all figured out. I can assure you that they don't. Nobody does. Even OpenAI CEO Sam Altman has said: "No one knows what happens next. I think the way technology goes; predictions are often wrong."[22]

So, we all must learn to accept that something new is always lurking around the corner. We'll need to become more comfortable with the uncomfortable speed of these technology hyper-cycles. We can't control the constant onslaught of change. So, one of my recommendations is to take a deep breath.

Feel better? Good. (I do too!) But now is the time to prepare. On a practical level, you need to control what you can control. You must get your technology house in order. This isn't a moment to keep saying, "Well, we're trying to transform our operations digitally, and by Q2 of next year…" It's go time, right now!

AI-readiness requires understanding your architecture and processes, getting your applications finally talking to one another, and ensuring your data is accessible. If you don't accomplish that first, pretrained generative transformers, large language models, and everything else AI will become just more "stuff" in your overly complex tech stack. You won't see the business value. Instead, you will fall behind your competitors – some of whom might not yet exist.

Even as so much is changing, one thing hasn't: Garbage in, garbage out. So much of the emphasis on AI revolves around chatbots, LLMs, and graphics processing units. But *data* is the fuel for an AI engine.

You need seamless access to your proprietary business data to train and continuously fine-tune your AI models. That means finding, transporting, enriching, cleaning, standardizing, and transforming your data. Only then will you have the contextualized data to "ground" those AI models to improve their accuracy and performance.

That ability to calibrate models requires a single, independent (you could also say "agnostic" or "unbiased" here) integration layer between systems that allows you to orchestrate and automate processes.

In an environment of innovative unpredictability, the best way to prepare for changes you can't predict is to become as nimble, agile, and flexible as possible to be ready when they burst onto the scene. Connectivity does that. An integration and automation strategy that's thoughtful and balanced allows you to adapt to technological advances perpetually. The best opportunity to participate in the radical reshaping of the future is when you can:

- Connect everyone to everything.
- Tame technology fragmentation and complexity.
- Finally digitally transform your operations.
- Increase business speed, agility, and flexibility.
- Enable the practical use of AI solutions.

Solving problems caused by disconnection, fragmentation, and complexity requires a universal translator for technology systems that can integrate applications, databases, APIs, and AI.

35

One way I think about this is a quote often attributed to Nelson Mandela: "If you talk to a man in a language he understands, it goes to his head. If you talk to him in his own language, that goes to his heart." That sentiment resonates with me because only about half of the world's population can converse in more than one language, and just 20% of the American population is bilingual, according to the US Census Bureau.[23] The lack of a common language is clearly a problem in my vision of a more connected world.

Our business systems face the same issue. Technology landscapes are a Tower of Babel where nothing communicates well. If you try to solve that problem by manually integrating two systems, that's like hiring a translator who can only speak English and German. What if you then need to connect them to other systems? Do you keep hiring more interpreters who speak Spanish, French, Japanese, and so on? It doesn't seem practical. That's like hiring expensive IT developers with expertise in one specific coding language or system but unfamiliar with others. And something inevitably gets lost in translation.

A multilingual, any-to-any integration platform that can translate all technology languages is smarter. We will spend time in this book talking about *how* to connect systems. But to understand where we're heading, we must discuss where we are today. Over the past decade or so, tools have emerged that help integrate and automate the systems that are critical to your business operations. Known as integration platforms as a service (iPaaS), these tools simplify the complex task of connecting different systems, enabling smoother workflows and more efficient processes.

Analyst firm Gartner attached this name to the software category. Gartner's observation, to a degree, is that iPaaS acts like a universal translator for your technology systems, ensuring everything from your CRM to your legacy systems can communicate effectively.

It simplifies integration, making it easier to automate workflows and ensure that the right data gets to the right place at the right time.

Here's exactly how Gartner describes the comprehensive capabilities of iPaaS and why they're an essential connectivity tool in today's business landscape:

Many technology categories help integrate systems together. Application integration suites, data integration tools, business process automation, and B2B gateway software are the four major integration software categories to enable most integration use cases. Other tools, such as low-code application platforms, can also provide a limited set of integration capabilities, but mostly for their own use of connected data and services. Of course, you can always code or script integrations, but that brings with it a whole different set of challenges. iPaaS addresses all these traditionally separate integration markets and has become the most popular approach for modern integration delivery.[24]

But let's not dwell on the term or an analyst firm's view of the world. System and data integration goes by many names. Some people call it "hyperautomation." (The automation of automation.) Others call it a data fabric or data mesh.

The goal is to ensure systems within a digital architecture can easily connect and communicate, which goes a long way toward eradicating architectural complexity. Foundational systems such as SAP, Microsoft, ServiceNow, Workday, Salesforce, Oracle, and others can finally "speak" in a common language. There's a need for something like a Google Translate for technology because:

- IT teams, whose jobs are harder than ever due to digital fragmentation, must have a standardized mechanism to quickly integrate systems and create a unified data layer that acts as connective tissue for the entire company.

From Chaos to Cohesion: Mastering AI-Driven Transformation

- Users in the lines of business want to more actively contribute their creativity by working on projects requiring system integration and process automation with an easy-to-use, no-code/low-code tool that abstracts away the technical complexity.

- Organizations seek to remove unnecessary friction from their operations so everyone can focus on doing their best work and satisfying customers.

Enter iPaaS. At its core, iPaaS connects essential systems and data within your organization so they work together seamlessly. iPaaS not only automates workflows but also plays a critical role in successful digital transformation. As AI becomes more integral to business operations, having a robust integration platform will help future-proof your organization.

This is the direction I want to guide you toward. But I'm getting a little ahead of myself. My point here is this: *Connectivity is the key to overcoming digital fragmentation and achieving true transformation.*

I have yet to see a company where connecting systems, processes, and people won't lead to better outcomes. Connection changes everything. Connection makes the world a better place.

Chapter Takeaway

Three Things to Know

1. Most digital transformation projects fall short of expectations, primarily due to the lack of connected systems and data.
2. Digital transformation isn't a one-and-done. It's an iterative process, and ongoing organizational flexibility, agility, and adaptability are basic requirements.

---

3. The AI era is changing everything. Integration and automation will be essential for businesses to navigate the coming changes and get the most from AI.

Why It Matters

Becoming an AI-ready business starts by connecting essential systems and ensuring easy access to crucial, trusted, real-time data.

The Bottom Line

The best way to prepare for changes you can't predict is to make your organization as nimble and flexible as possible. This requires a relentless focus on integration and automation. The actual outcome is making your organization more agile, cost-efficient, and able to deliver on your promises to customers. When all this happens, you increase your ability to improve lives by making people healthier, wealthier, and happier.

Chapter 2

Integration: Uniting Systems to End Fragmentation

What we discuss in this chapter:

- How CIOs face the supreme challenge of connecting systems and databases in today's fragmented digital architectures.

- A closer look at the many factors contributing to application disconnection and how a lack of integration prevents business success.

- The American Cancer Society (ACS) provides help and hope to people fighting the disease with an IT strategy of connecting systems and automating processes.

"We remove barriers and reduce the burden while people go through their cancer journeys."

The word alone is terrifying: *cancer.* Especially if a doctor has just broken the overwhelming news that you have a form of the potentially deadly disease, and you're suddenly facing your mortality.

"When you're notified you have cancer, that's kind of where your mind shuts off," said Ricky Koch, the CIO of the American Cancer Society. "It's just too much to process everything. We come in after that moment. We help people navigate what comes next and try to make this not as tough because they're already stressed out after the diagnosis."

For more than 110 years, the American Cancer Society[25] has strived to end cancer as we know it – for everyone. But ensuring the prevention, detection, treatment, and survival of cancer is a monumental task due to the sheer scope of the disease. In the United States, 1 in 2 men and 1 in 3 women will be diagnosed with cancer in their lifetime.[26]

The nonprofit's mission is to change that. The impact of the organization's efforts is breathtaking:

- **Research:** Since 1946, $5 billion has been invested in cancer research, contributing to a 33% decline in cancer death rates from 1991 to 2021.

- **Support for patients and caregivers:** In 2023, the organization's efforts touched 152 million lives.

- **Fundraising:** $8 billion has been raised since 1985 to provide money for programs and research.

- **Advocacy:** Lobbying efforts to influence public health policy have prioritized the fight against cancer and increased awareness about issues like early detection.

But the American Cancer Society's direct impact on lives is what tugs at heartstrings. The ACS Cares mobile app provides personalized answers for people with questions. There's also a 24/7 hotline when people need to talk to someone. Koch shared that the organization provided more than 47,000 rides in the Road to Recovery program in 2023 alone, where people needing lifesaving cancer treatment were matched with volunteers to get them to and from appointments. Also, more than 500,000 nights of accommodation a year are provided at Hope Lodges so people can stay near their treatment centers.

"If you're not wealthy, there's a lot of barriers out there to getting cancer treatment," Koch said. "It shouldn't be that way. We remove barriers and reduce the burden while people go through their cancer journeys."

Delivering these kinds of services requires managing an incredible amount of data. That's where an AI-driven integration and automation platform plays a role. The organization initially implemented the Boomi Enterprise Platform during a digital modernization project to eliminate legacy systems that had become too costly to maintain or upgrade and weren't meeting the needs of staff, volunteers, and patients. Today, the platform connects digital operations with over 250 integrations, including Salesforce, NetSuite, and other critical systems such as procurement and event planning.

This connectivity gives the American Cancer Society an accurate picture of expenses, donations, volunteer activities, advocacy to government officials, and who is reaching out for services. It also assists the organization in operating a travel booking center with its Hope Lodge network and a rideshare operation like Lyft or Uber to connect volunteers and patients.

"For us, it's all about helping every cancer patient, but also having all that data to know what we've done and how we've done it," Koch added. "The integration piece is how that flows through systems."

Koch joined the American Cancer Society more than two decades ago after working in the insurance industry because the organization's mission deeply resonates with him. Koch watched his mother-in-law endure chemotherapy treatments in her cancer fight. Knowing, statistically speaking, one of his two daughters or wife might also be diagnosed with cancer someday drives him to ensure the research they fund keeps making advances and everyone has easy access to treatment.

As a CIO, Koch confronts the same challenges as every technical leader: more projects, systems, and data than people. The platform helps his team get more done by easily connecting systems and automating processes. He estimates that if they had to build and manage their current integrations with labor-intensive coding, it might require an additional 20–30 people. That efficiency and optimization ensures less money gets spent on operations and more goes to services.

"My whole goal is to reduce IT as a cost center and ensure more money is put into the mission," he said. "I think about it in simple terms. How many more beakers can you buy with an additional $5? How many more nights can we provide in a lodge stay if I save $100?"

That watchful eye on expenses helps explain why the American Cancer Society is a Better Business Bureau-accredited charity, meeting all 20 standards for accountability.[27]

Koch said the organization also embraces AI, with several pilot projects in development. He's excited about AI's natural language capabilities. He believes it will lead to more personalized and easier-to-understand answers when people search to answer questions. Today, the answers to Internet queries about cancer can be confusing with arcane medical terminology.

"I believe removing the literacy barrier will be just another way we can help people," Koch said. "That's our whole mission – helping."

Key Points

- **Goal:** Lead the fight against cancer by ensuring that staff and volunteers always have access to the data that provides the best information and services for people coping with the disease.

- **Human Impact:** The Boomi Enterprise Platform is integral to the American Cancer Society's mission. In 2024, the organization processed as many as 92,000 transactions in a single day. Also, the Road to Recovery rideshare program averaged between 5,200 and 5,500 rides monthly, so cancer patients had access to treatment.

- **Lessons Learned:** "We've learned to bite off smaller pieces with our integrations, get them working well, and then expand. The benefit of that agile approach is you can see where your mistakes are, quickly fix them, and adjust. That eases the communication struggle between the technical and business teams. When they ask for a car, they want to see a car. They don't want to see a chassis and then hear you say 'once that's right, we'll put on the hood, the engine, and everything else.' But if we build a smaller integration with a small amount of data, we can get that flowing and understand our errors. That solves a lot of problems when you're facing complicated challenges. It's just made everything a lot smoother."
  – *Ricky Koch, CIO, American Cancer Society*

The CIO's Dilemma

This story hits home for me. When I was first diagnosed with Type 1 diabetes, the support from my family and friends was my lifeline. The thought of someone facing a life-threatening illness like cancer, which is profoundly scarier than Type 1 diabetes, without that kind of support – or even a ride to treatment – is gut-wrenching. The way the American Cancer Society bridges that gap is a powerful testament to the strength of connection.

As a technologist, I often think about how access to data could help in the fight to end cancer. Consider the thousands of systems with critical health and treatment data distributed across hundreds of thousands of researchers and millions of doctors all over the world. I realize the immense regulatory hurdles involved in bringing that information together. But, to dream for just a moment, what if we could connect it all? This is why I believe in integration platforms.

45

Ricky Koch's insight about AI's potential to deliver better answers also resonates deeply with me. I've been in that position, frantically searching the Internet for clarity on my condition, only to find myself lost in a maze of confusing information. AI's ability to transform those desperate searches into clear, actionable answers is one of the most thrilling promises of this technology.

But there's another layer to this story: the immense responsibility that CIOs bear in today's digital landscape. They are the unsung heroes tasked with weaving together the complex tapestry of our digital ecosystems. In my view, CIOs hold the most challenging role in modern business. They're expected to ensure that everything runs smoothly and securely, yet they no longer have full control over the technology within their organizations.

Larry Quinlan, former global chief information officer of Deloitte and current board member for several companies, has an interesting way of explaining this new reality: "The genie is out of the bottle." IT is no longer calling all the shots because of the democratization of technology assets.

"The days of the CIO overseeing the writing of every line of code are over," Larry told me. "You have everyone in the organization wanting to contribute their creativity. But that also means when you have everyone involved, it can lead to chaos. Everything is no longer centralized, and IT is not in control of everything."

Anyone inside an IT organization knows this. Lines of business are more empowered than ever to get whatever applications they want, whether or not they connect back to the company's technology or data strategies. For example, maybe the head of sales says: "We're going to use this application because I heard that it's great!" But the CIO has to think about how that app will work with the company's security policies and how it ties into the overall data approach. The CIO also doesn't know if the business will still use that application when another new head of sales takes over. However, the ultimatum of making it work still stands regardless of the open questions.

Once upon a time, IT had significantly more organizational control and authority. That's because, as Larry noted, systems were centralized. (Thank you, mainframe and client/server.) IT made decisions, and the rest of the business followed. But this has changed with the advent of cloud computing. Lines of business now can easily make their own technology decisions about what's best suited for their needs. Today, for instance, IT rarely initiates the implementation of CRM systems such as Salesforce. Instead, this starts with business users who are dissatisfied with the existing CRM and want something new. The pendulum has swung totally to the lines of businesses when selecting applications. Now, IT has to follow. I'm not advocating for or against this approach. This is just the reality.

Sometimes, the term "Shadow IT" is appropriate because the technical team doesn't have a complete picture of what's in the software stack. But in a general sense, I think that phrase is simply a way for IT to grudgingly describe a process where business units dictate the selection process. IT teams know an app is being used. They just didn't get a vote on its presence. Either way, the digital ecosystem has become the wild, wild west. The CIO, playing the sheriff's role, is left struggling to keep order and ensure everything fits within the overall architecture.

Any new CIO begins the job by trying to understand their actual scope of authority. Does their team have a voice in selecting business applications? Or is their role only to choose the technologies that IT explicitly needs? Most CIOs are walking into a hodgepodge of operations. Some are owned and operated by IT. The likelihood, though, is that the majority were selected by a myriad of business units. And guess who has to spot-weld those technologies into the broader infrastructure? That would be the lucky CIO!

Integration: Uniting Systems to End Fragmentation

The job of running IT can be thankless. In most cases, digital fragmentation is the culprit. The CIO's team must figure out how to connect all those applications, so data can be shared and teams can collaborate effectively. They must fit them into the company's data model to provide a unified, company-wide view. After integrating systems, IT has to maintain those connections as organizations inevitably change and evolve. And now, they also have to adapt to AI. Oh, and they're expected to cut costs somehow while they're at it. Awesome.

Keeping everything together requires a lot of glue. The amount can depend on the organization's approach to digital architecture: Is it homogeneous or heterogeneous? There's no right answer – each presents different structural obstacles to creating a connected ecosystem.

The Road to Fragmentation

It's important to note that I use the word "fragmentation" as a substitution for the phrase "unintegrated systems that drive chaos and inefficiency." It also reflects what happens to businesses over time when different divisions, departments, groups, and, yes, applications don't talk to each other. So, we will stick with "fragmentation" throughout the book.

In this vein, let's first consider homogeneous technology architectures.

I've mentioned that my resume includes experiences at some of the world's biggest and best technology companies: SAP, Salesforce, Microsoft, and Adobe. Of course, all these tech giants aim to sell more products and services. They're very good at it. With this in mind, it's not in their best interests to design software that easily talks with other systems – at least not as part of its core functionality. They would rather sell more of their stuff than help you connect their software to somebody else's technology. So, these companies have a self-serving, economic incentive to create tech gardens with high walls. And there's absolutely nothing wrong with this. That's capitalism. But it also means every vendor wants your data in their platform.

In the software business, "stickiness" is everything. It makes sense because the longer you hold a subscription, the more profitable the customer. Another consideration is that landing new customers is *expensive* – typically three times more costly than getting existing ones to buy more. That's why we work hard to keep our customers happy and deeply embedded in our ecosystems.

Megavendors aim to make their platforms indispensable, encouraging customers to buy more add-ons to the core systems. They know once you're in, it's painful, costly, and time-consuming to rip out and replace these platforms. This creates that "stickiness." But it can also lead to being locked into a megavendor's vision, even if it's not the best fit for your needs. This much is clear: The idea of a single platform that fits all needs is a myth. No vendor – whether SAP, Oracle, or Microsoft – can fulfill every requirement.

While these systems excel within their ecosystems, they weren't built to communicate easily with others. Oracle doesn't speak SAP, SAP doesn't speak Microsoft, and so on. (Been there, lived that for three decades myself.) Even if these vendors claim to be open and accessible, true seamless connectivity is rare. They don't prioritize making data flow freely across different systems, and that mindset creates significant integration challenges.

On the flip side, the rise of best-of-breed cloud applications has driven a shift toward more heterogeneous architectures. Here, companies choose the best tools for specific needs rather than relying on a single vendor. This approach offers greater flexibility and allows for more tailored solutions, especially in areas like ERP systems, which are the financial heart of any organization. But this strategy also adds a familiar problem: integration. The more specialized applications you add, the more difficult it becomes to connect them all.

Gartner calls this the "Composable Enterprise Era," in which organizations mix and match applications and microservices to solve specific problems.[28] It's a more flexible, modular approach, but it comes at the cost of increased connectivity complexity.

To sum up, whether you're sticking to a *single vendor* or adopting a *best-of-breed approach*, you'll face integration headaches. The tug-of-war between uniformity and diversity in application landscapes has always led to one inevitable challenge: making everything work together smoothly.

Both scenarios result in the same problem: None of these things freaking talk to one another!

But like most things in life, digital architectures aren't an either-or scenario. Today, organizations fall somewhere in the middle of a broad scale with hybrid architectures. This means they have:

- Core on-premises systems and data centers behind firewalls
- Multiple public clouds or a hybrid environment with private and public clouds
- A broad diversity of SaaS applications
- Edge devices and sensors
- Database storage lakes and warehouses

Soon, they will also have multi-AI models, but I get to that in a later chapter.

These bullet points don't represent a comprehensive list. However, they capture many prominent places where data resides and must be easily accessible. They also illustrate the reason for data sprawl. Hybrid architectures with a patchwork of isolated systems are the reality in today's world, and they're growing in scale and complexity.

Remember how we discussed in the previous chapter that the typical organization uses an average of 342 SaaS applications? Let's consider just marketers for a moment. Their teams have become ravenous consumers of software. The expansion of marketing tech was well underway back when I ran the marketing automation company Marketo, and it continues today. Scott Brinker is an astute observer of the growth trend, and his 2024 Marketing Technology Landscape Supergraphic looks like an eye chart nightmare with an astounding 14,106 solutions available.[29] It shows 27.8% growth in the number of available marketing solutions in just one year.

Marketers may buy those digital tools, but IT teams must manage them. That's just one department, mind you. Stacks of technologies throughout the business sit atop one another. Connecting them with traditional one-to-one integrations requires extensive effort by high-priced developers to hand-code and maintain. If you think back to the technology landscape graphic I referred to earlier, you now understand why that looks the way it does.

I also used the analogy of complex digital architecture looking like a subway map. That's the lay of the land within most companies. It's no wonder businesses often feel that the technologies they buy overpromise and underperform. Also, data is not only everywhere, but it resides in systems introduced decades apart. This is why digital landscapes can also be compared to urban environments.

Think about the skylines of the world's great cities, such as New York, San Francisco, Sydney, or London. There's a sharp contrast between the look and feel of building construction. You might have the utilitarian-style architecture of the 1960s and 1970s one block away from gleaming, modern glass skyscrapers. There's no such thing as uniformity, and that's part of the charm of cities – the vibrancy of diversity.

But all too often, we celebrate architects who design a single, iconic building while not heaping enough praise on the urban planners who make entire cities operate smoothly. These are the behind-the-scenes people who think about electricity, water, and safe streets – the things that make cities great places to live and work. The best planners understand that cities can't scale without connected infrastructure.

It's the same with technology. There's no such thing as uniformity when it comes to systems and applications. They were added at different times to handle disparate needs. Connecting everything and ensuring the entire architecture – as well as all the individual components – is scalable can be incredibly challenging.

The Problems Caused by Fragmentation

Fragmentation in your business systems isn't just an inconvenience – it's a ticking time bomb. Poor connectivity and disjointed data create a domino effect of inefficiencies and risks that can cripple your operations. If any, or worse, *all* the following real-world fragmentation scenarios listed below apply to your company, it's a red flag that you're in desperate need of an integration platform.

- **Sales:** Without real-time customer information, you miss opportunities, duplicate efforts, and make poor decisions. Flawed forecasting and reporting are just the start – every misstep gives your competitors an edge.

- **Marketing:** Inaccurate targeting and inconsistent messaging weaken your campaigns. When your marketing doesn't hit the mark, your brand reputation suffers, and so does customer trust.

- **IT:** Rising maintenance costs, endless data reconciliation, and constant troubleshooting strain your resources. Even worse, gaps in data protection open the door to security risks, making your business an easier target for attacks.

- **Supply Chain Management:** Poor visibility leads to inventory issues – such as stockouts, overstocking, and shipment delays. These problems ripple through your operations, resulting in frustrated customers.

- **Customer Support:** Service agents struggle to respond quickly and accurately without the right insights. Longer resolution times and lack of personalization can cause dissatisfaction and customers to seek alternatives – your competitors.

- **Finance:** Difficulty reconciling accounts leads to inaccurate financial reporting, which disrupts budgeting, forecasting, and cost control. You may make decisions that could harm your business without a clear financial picture.

- **Risk, Compliance, and Auditing:** The inability to minimize human errors and respond quickly to issues increases the risk of noncompliance, fraud, and higher costs. These problems can spiral out of control, leading to expensive mistakes and regulatory fines.

- **Human Resources:** Recruitment and retention efforts stall when data isn't connected. Delays in sourcing candidates, poor collaboration with hiring managers, and a lack of unified employee data make it harder to attract and keep top talent.

- **Operations:** Inefficiencies caused by poor visibility into resource planning, scheduling, and asset allocation drive up costs and cause delays. Without integrated systems, you can't optimize or automate, leading to missed opportunities and wasted resources.

- **Product Development and Engineering:** Poor collaboration between teams leads to delays, cost overruns, and quality issues. When systems don't talk to each other, innovation slows down, and your products suffer.

- **Procurement:** Errors and delays in processing orders, approvals, and payments create bottlenecks that can result in missed deadlines, financial penalties, and even legal risks.

These issues are the day-to-day headaches that result from poor connectivity. But the bigger picture is even more concerning. Fragmentation can also lead to the following:

- **Poor Decision-Making:** Out-of-date or inaccurate information undermines your strategic planning, leading to decisions based on flawed data.

- **Poor Customer Experience:** Disconnected systems prevent you from gaining a complete view of your customers, making it impossible to understand their needs and deliver the experiences they expect.

- **Hindrances to Innovation and Growth:** Siloed data and fragmented systems slow collaboration, making it harder to innovate and grow your business efficiently.

- **Risk Management Challenges:** Poorly integrated systems create blind spots in recordkeeping, security, and compliance, exposing you to fraud and regulatory issues.

- **Low Employee Productivity and Satisfaction:** You risk losing talent and lowering overall morale without the data to understand what your employees need.

- **Competitive Disadvantage:** Without the agility to pivot quickly, your business falls behind competitors who are more connected and better equipped to adapt.

If your business is facing these challenges, it's time to consider an integration platform. Connectivity isn't just a nice-to-have. It's essential for your business to thrive.

The Long-Running Battle Against Fragmentation

Back in the 1990s, one of my favorite operations in Microsoft's Windows suite was the disk defragmenter tool for cleaning up the hard drive. You would run it to locate fragmented data and then store it properly to save disk space. I found it quite cathartic watching it clean up the computer. (For those too young to know about this, check out a YouTube video.)

I mention this because, in a manner of speaking, we've been trying to "defragment" our digital architecture for as long as we've used computers within our businesses. We've used a wide assortment of technologies attempting to knit together our systems and exchange information. The oldest (and most inefficient) method is simple text and flat files. If I had some data that I wanted to share with you, but my system didn't talk to your system, I would just take a text file and manually dump it into your system.

Over the years, information-sharing approaches have continuously evolved. The methods we've used have changed dramatically. Each has brought its own set of challenges and benefits. Therefore, I humbly submit to you "Steve's Top 10 Ways to Integrate and Share Data." (You might want to bookmark this so you can refer to it later when we discuss modern integration platforms in depth.)

1. **Text and Flat Files:** The old-school method mentioned previously, where I would dump my data into a text file and send it your way. Simple, but about as modern as fax machines.

Integration: Uniting Systems to End Fragmentation

2. **Electronic Data Interchange (EDI):** The granddaddy of digital communication that has been swapping business data since the 1960s. It's still reliable and still relevant.[30]

3. **Point-to-Point Integrations:** Custom-built connections that are as time-consuming as they are fragile. Change anything, and you're back to the drawing board.

4. **Enterprise Service Bus (ESB):** The middleware giant that tried to be the one-stop-shop for integration but ended up being more complex and sluggish than expected.

5. **Application Programming Interfaces (APIs):** The digital connectors that ensure different systems play nicely together. APIs are the behind-the-scenes MVPs of the global economy.

6. **Extract, Transform, Load (ETL):** The data-moving trio that gets your data from Point A to Point B, with a pit stop for transformation. ELT is the "let's deal with it later" sibling.

7. **Robotic Process Automation (RPA):** Your digital minions that handle the boring, repetitive tasks no one wants to do. Tireless, but also slightly robotic.

8. **Event-Driven Integration:** The real-time responder that jumps into action whenever something important happens. Fast, efficient, and always on its toes.

9. **Data Warehousing:** The centralized hub where all your data comes to live, breathe, and interact. It's where the magic of big data happens.

10. **Integration Platform as a Service (iPaaS):** The modern answer to all your integration needs, handling connections like a pro and making sure everything talks to everything else seamlessly.

Bonus Honorable Mention: SOAP, REST, B2B Gateways, Message Queues, Service-Oriented Architecture (SOA)

Each of these methods has played a role in the ongoing effort to defragment our digital architectures, enabling businesses to connect systems, automate processes, and create a smooth flow of data. As technology continues to advance, so too will the methods we use to integrate our systems and unlock the full potential of our digital ecosystems.

High-Performance Engines Need High-Performance Connectivity

I love everything about cars. I view them as moving art. I see beauty in every vehicle. One of my hobbies is finding ways to make them go fast.[31] My son and I spend our free time in the garage, restoring and upgrading high-end cars. The fastest I've ever driven is 203 mph. (I should also emphasize that I was on a Formula 1-certified race-course with a professional driver in the car coaching me.)

Metaphors involving race cars are excellent ways to highlight critical business points. If you were ever to attend one of my company's all-hands events, you might very well hear me say that there's a reason why windshields are so much bigger than rear-view mirrors. That's because paying attention to what's ahead of us is more important than looking backward.

Here's another one. Investing in a foundational technology system like SAP for your business is like purchasing a high-performance engine. It gives you sheer horsepower with information about customers, vendors, supply chains, products, financials, etc. You're willing to invest vast amounts of money and resources into that engine because it can be the difference between your car – the business – reaching the checkered flag first or finishing in the middle of the pack.

57

But do you also have the kind of tires that will ensure you can win the race? In this metaphor, the tires represent connectivity.

If you're in a business race against ruthless competition, it's a mistake to invest in the technology power under the hood of a Porsche or Ferrari and then slap on cheap tires from the local big box store. That's literally where the rubber meets the road. As someone who has been in minor crashes on racetracks, you very quickly appreciate the value of a great tire. In business, cheap tires will put you into a wall. Just as a car's performance is only as good as the tires it sits on; a technology architecture is only as good as its connectivity.

Yet integration is often relegated to an afterthought when choosing the technologies to run our operations. Not enough consideration is directed toward an essential question: "How are we going to connect this to everything else?"

Some people will say that all software tastes like chicken. I'm not in that camp. There's an incredible variety of technologies out there. So, the most obvious notion I have ever encountered in software is having a single, comprehensive way for disparate applications and databases to speak to one another. You need a *lingua franca*. For humans, that's communication in a third language when two people don't share a native language. It's the same for digital systems. That's an obvious conclusion that should be clear to every CIO. But it's also maddeningly frustrating that this translation doesn't just happen.

Before a technical leader starts thinking about foundational systems, applications, databases, and everything else (hello, AI models!), they should start with something more fundamental: deciding how all these systems, apps, and tools will talk to each other. Yet the reality is that business and technical leaders rarely consider that problem until it's too late, which goes a long way toward explaining digital fragmentation.

The very first thing a CIO should think about is an integration strategy. Why? Regardless of what systems you have, *how* you connect things (e.g. people, applications, data, and processes) matters most. Systems come and go. But if you, as an IT leader, can present a unified front for data, applications, and APIs, you win. It's like an abstraction layer for your business users because they don't need to see how things are made!

For me, a best-of-breed ethos is the better approach for modern organizations. But every business is different, and maybe you've settled on an SAP suite, an Oracle suite, or it-doesn't-matter suite. It's the same principle regardless of your architecture. You must replace the complex plate of spaghetti point-to-point integrations with a unified, horizontal, and scalable "layer of connectivity" that integrates everything in a composable architecture with an interoperable interface.

You need a hyper-nimble connection layer for two reasons:

1. You can't rely on software vendors to provide plug-and-play connectivity because it will never happen at the speed and agility required for you to stay ahead of your competitors. Every application vendor believes integration is somebody else's problem and expects you to figure out how to stitch the pieces together.

2. A unified, lightweight integration layer that requires little or no coding simplifies the old, time-consuming process of stitching System A to System B together with a brittle, code-heavy connection. In today's world, one-to-one connectivity will break your business. It can't even be one-to-many. It has to be any-to-any.

Larry Quinlan, the former Deloitte CIO I quoted earlier, says, "You need a platform that connects everything and creates an environment where everyone can thrive and accomplish their aspirations."

Integration: Uniting Systems to End Fragmentation

He's right. The advent of the cloud and hybrid architectures has brought us so much innovation. But for the CIO, life is exponentially more difficult because there's so much more complexity. That's why another concept you often hear in IT is the term "single pane of glass." This is the idea of consolidating all the varied software systems, applications, and tools into one interface where you can manage everything with complete visibility. When that happens, you have greater efficiency, better decision-making, and improved overall system performance.

Of course, that's usually more of an aspirational goal. But it does explain why iPaaS emerged to fill that gap. A single platform to connect and automate everything is vital to creating digital cohesion.

The Power of a Connectivity Layer

In the last chapter, we briefly touched on iPaaS. Once again, I urge you not to become overly fixated on that acronym. I know that's hard because, in software, there's a love of emphasizing buzzwords. Candidly, I find that term quite limiting. But humans love to slap labels on things, and this one stuck. What's more important here is thinking about the concept of using a single platform to connect everything.

iPaaS is more than just a set of digital tools – it's an approach. It's the connective tissue that binds together your digital architecture, seamlessly weaving together application and data integration, ETL, API management, processes, and more (Figure 2.1). As integration needs have evolved, so has the platform, expanding to meet the demands of a rapidly changing business landscape. The result? A flexible framework that gives you the freedom to connect your data and applications however you see fit.

Every CIO knows the IT landscape is a jungle of fragmented systems and tangled data. And to tame it, you need a lightweight, versatile tool that can connect everything. This is where a common

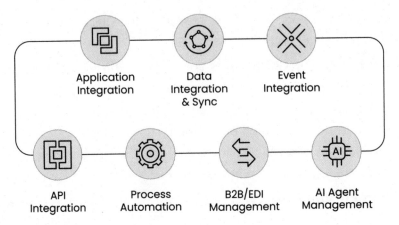

Figure 2.1 Integration Platform as a Service (iPaaS) architecture.

integration layer comes into play. It's the key to eliminating fragmentation, reducing architectural complexity, and driving operational excellence by:

- **Bringing all the elements of system integration and automation under one roof:** Whether it's data, applications, devices, API management, EDI, or workflow automation, this approach ensures you can meet any integration pattern or automation need. It's like having a Swiss Army knife for your IT environment.

- **Creating seamless connectivity across disparate environments:** Whether on premises, in the cloud, or at the edge, a unified integration platform breaks down internal data silos and connects you with partners, vendors, and other third parties. It's about making sure every part of your ecosystem can talk to each other – no matter where it lives.

- **Reducing the need for technical skills with a low-code/ no-code solution:** This empowers your business users to take a more active role in overseeing projects, speeding up development, and easing the burden on IT. It's about bridging the

Integration: Uniting Systems to End Fragmentation

divide between IT and business to foster a more collaborative, efficient working relationship.

- **Providing visibility into your entire digital architecture:** Understanding what's in your ecosystem is crucial, especially for meeting security challenges. A 2024 World Economic Forum article rightly pointed out that digital fragmentation makes life easier for cybercriminals.[32] A common integration layer helps you lock those doors and keep your data safe.

- **Controlling costs by getting more out of legacy systems:** Integration isn't just about moving forward. It's also about making sure the systems you've invested in continue to deliver value. Forrester Consulting found that integration can breathe new life into legacy systems, allowing you to avoid costly rip-and-replace projects while still moving toward a modern, cloud-native architecture.[33]

- **Containing digital transformation costs:** Integration platforms streamline processes, reducing overall cloud spending and improving efficiencies across the board. Another 2024 survey from Forrester Consulting found that 67% of corporate decision-makers observed reduced cloud costs thanks to their integration platform.[34]

- **Ensuring data accessibility to power AI initiatives:** As AI becomes increasingly essential, having structured, unstructured, and semi-structured data readily available is critical for building an AI-ready architecture.

In our fragmented software world, a platform with multiple capabilities is crucial to cutting through the chaos. The keyword to remember is "one." You don't want to solve your integration problems with a dozen different solutions. This doesn't solve anything. What you need is one platform that does it all.

While the idea of uniting business systems is universally agreed upon, it remains one of the toughest challenges for technology leaders. Reducing the number of systems, applications, and databases might not be realistic, but creating a single integration layer is. This approach simplifies your architecture, ensures everything is connected, and paves the way for a more streamlined, effective business operation.

This is why integration and automation must be central to your strategy. Downplaying their importance as mere "IT plumbing" is a recipe for disaster. When done right, a connectivity strategy is the secret sauce that makes everything else work. When your technologies work together, your organization becomes more productive. And your customers will thank you for it.

Recall how I promised you would hear from renowned business and technology leaders on the topics we tackle in this book? I've already mentioned Larry Quinlan a couple of times in this chapter. More from a conversation I had with Larry – who in my opinion is the epitome of the modern CIO – is up next.

Chapter Takeaway

Three Things to Know

1. Data and application fragmentation is an age-old problem, mainly because even though systems may evolve and advance, they still aren't being designed to communicate with one another.
2. Systems integration is often an afterthought, leading to disappointing results in critical technology initiatives.

(continued)

(continued)

3. Regardless of your business's digital architecture strategy, connecting everything within your technology landscape should be your top priority.

Why It Matters

At a time when CIOs and their teams have the most challenging jobs within businesses, they must have the right tools to help them limit the scope of digital fragmentation.

The Bottom Line

A single connectivity layer is the best way to limit digital fragmentation. Replacing a mishmash of point-to-point integrations with a unified platform allows you to choose the integration patterns you prefer and simplifies your architecture.

A Conversation with Larry Quinlan

■ ■ ■

No one understands the role of a Chief Information Officer better than Larry Quinlan. As the former global CIO for Deloitte, he was responsible for the $45-billion professional services firm's technology strategy and operations, managing over 10,000 IT professionals in 175 countries.

Yet even those numbers don't capture the demands of that role. Larry was responsible for one of the world's most advanced technology infrastructures. It needed to support a cutting-edge workforce around tax and auditing expertise and Deloitte's technology consulting arm. Perhaps most importantly, Larry's team needed to be a shining example of IT excellence for Deloitte customers with zero downtime and failure-is-not-an-option infrastructure. Somehow, though, he made it look easy.

With over 35 years of experience advising Fortune 500 boards and CEOs, Larry has a unique understanding of the strategic impacts of emerging technologies. He sits on numerous company boards today and is an eloquent advocate for diversity and career growth by encouraging people to become more persuasive champions of their abilities within organizations.

He's incredibly thoughtful about digital transformation, the significant changes that modern CIOs face, and how technologists can prepare for AI's growing impact. But what's perhaps most inspiring about Larry, and why I respect him so much, is his sincere belief the most essential element of technology is how it affects people.

Steve Lucas: If I say "digital transformation," what comes to mind?

Larry Quinlan: It's one of those terms that could mean whatever you want. It could be a CEO directive at a global enterprise level. Or it could be a basic implementation of something for a small department of workers. The CEOs who have set out to truly digitize their businesses with enterprise-wide goals understand the notion of taking friction out of processes, reducing costs in processes, and making life easier for people while also increasing the top line by reducing customer attrition, etc. The problem is it's time-consuming. It's expensive. And people go into it with this naivete that it will get done this year. They're shocked when it turns into a multiyear slog. Computers can change a lot of stuff, but people change things more. Transformation requires a true commitment to people. But too often, we just want to put in a system and say, "We're done."

SL: I imagine you oversaw many major digital initiatives during your tenure at Deloitte. Do any of them stand out for you?

LQ: The notable ones fall into different buckets. There are system implementations like ERPs, SAP, and Salesforce. There are productivity implementations like Microsoft Teams and Zoom. Then, there are large implementations with lines of business for something like tax processing software or a large audit platform. There are also things like developer productivity tools and security implementations. What's notable is the ones that succeed are tightly tied to human beings.

SL: OK, now that got my attention. I asked you about technology, and you turned the question around to talk about people. I want to hear more.

LQ: I know it sounds heretical, but forget the enterprise for a moment. Instead, ask yourself, "How will this initiative make life easier for the actual people who have to use it?" – whether it's for someone driving a truck, accessing a banking system, or using a help desk. Did we make their lives better? We don't integrate systems just to do it. We need to integrate them because by doing so, we can demonstrably prove that someone can do the task faster than before, and we don't make them tear their hair out in frustration. Here's an example. Implementing automation on a help desk seems to make people happy because they can now do something like update their credit card information faster on their own. But what if they make a mistake, and there's no way to get a human being to fix it? A small problem has mushroomed into a big one, and now everybody's totally upset. Transformation requires thinking about outcomes. Those outcomes have to do with how people feel about the changes we've made.

SL: If I understand what you're saying correctly, digital for the sake of digital without considering the human element is essentially empty.

LQ: It's much worse than empty. It actually creates failure – expensive failure. It makes people redo or delay projects and maybe spend millions in the process. Jobs are lost. Careers get stalled. It has a truly negative impact. When we do these big digital implementations, we can either make a mess of something, make it a neutral change, or really make a difference. For me, digital transformation is about making a real positive difference. That's different from just systems implementation.

A Conversation with Larry Quinlan

SL: I love that idea. So then, how essential are integration and automation to making any digital project a success?

LQ: They're absolutely critical elements for me. Digital transformation can't be successful without integration and automation. They're essential to achieving the stuff we're talking about – making humans more productive and streamlining processes. Transforming any major process in an organization requires integration. No executive wakes up each day knowing that all their processes are inside SAP, Oracle, or any other favorite system. It's not the way enterprises or people work. Decision-making requires constantly pulling information out of your HR system, your financial system, your supply chain system, etc. And it's hard. Those systems were built in different times, sometimes using different taxonomies. The whole notion of integration becomes essential if you're going to focus on the person.

SL: I want to double-click on that. You're really emphasizing the importance of the human element. Do you think IT organizations struggle with a focus on outcomes that impact real people?

LQ: Everybody struggles with it, not just IT. But first, IT organizations were not set up in the past to think like this. They were set up to take care of technology, not people. People were an unnecessary distraction. The old IT joke was, "My systems would work well if you stopped using them."

SL: You have to love a little IT humor. The easy part is what happens in the code. The hard part is when humans enter the equation.

LQ: But life has changed, Steve. If you look at the life of a CIO now, anything important the CIO wants to accomplish is totally dependent on other business units. Gone are the days when you simply ran an X.25 network if you wanted. You didn't care about what the business units wanted. The CIO just did it. But in today's world, in every process you want to implement and every system you want to put in, business units are fundamentally important. The people in those units are fundamentally important. So, the life of the CIO has fundamentally changed.

SL: What does that mean for businesses in the practical, day-to-day sense?

LQ: Many enterprises have just blown by their IT organizations. They want technology embedded in the business units, where it's closer to the action. But then, predictably, failure occurs in several different ways. They may succeed on the projects, but then every unit is doing something different. At some point, there's hell to pay because you're spending way too much money on systems, they don't talk to each other, etc. Then, there will be enterprise-level initiatives that you can't put in place because you have a hodgepodge of stuff. Or things fail because sometimes business units don't know what they're doing. I think the right answer isn't to blow by your IT organization. Instead, it's to completely transform and upgrade your IT organization with the kinds of CIOs and IT capabilities that understand what's needed. Your father's IT organization doesn't work anymore. IT needs to work very closely with business units. That's absolutely part of the job today.

SL: What do you think CIOs should consider as they integrate and automate their systems? What's the right "altitude" for you?

LQ: We still have CIOs who don't look at it from the altitude needed. They're looking at it on an operational level, just trying to get projects done so they don't get beat down. But you have modern CIOs who are strategic executives focused on big platforms and how those integrate. What's the method of integration? Which vendors do they trust? When do they have to write something themselves? Which ones should they buy? How does that come together? And how do you track success and know that something's working? How do you instrument it? How do you protect it? How do you create a platform that allows you to be successful, even if you aren't doing all of it yourself? All of that is what the best CIOs are considering. The enterprise is so completely dependent on technology now. You have to create a platform that allows other people to play on that platform yet gives you visibility, security, integration, automation, and all of those things. A modern CIO can't just get out of the way and let people do their own stuff because it will just come back to haunt you. You also can't be in the business anymore of just saying, "Hey, business unit. I've decided you will get a 2% increase in your IT budget, and when my developers get around to it, we'll help you."

SL: As you said, those days are long gone. Then, how do you see the role of a modern CIO?

LQ: The modern CIO's job is really to figure out how to work with all the business units and ensure what kinds of activities they can do on a platform that the CIO provides in a way that the CIO doesn't have to do every part of that project. A CIO also has to figure out how to protect the entire enterprise. That means being responsible for maintaining and securing all those connections. Everybody has either had a cyber incident or will have one. It's just reality. So, you've got to be able to say, where's my data? Where's it going? Where's it coming from? What would I expect the downstream impact to be? What systems are plugging into all of this?

SL: With the introduction of AI, large language models, generative pretrained transformers, and agents, do you think integration and automation become more important or less important?

LQ: Definitely more important, without a doubt. This whole AI phenomenon is about data. It's trained by data, feeds off data, and spits out data. Yes, there's some incredible hardware involved with AI. But for me, data is at the heart. So many organizations put out statements about everything they're going to do with AI. But many don't even know what data they have or where it is, and they have no integration-automation platform in place. The ability to marshal that data and train models to meet new regulations is crucial. You will have to defend your algorithms and demonstrate how you got to the answers you did. That traceability requires real discipline around data and becoming more capable with security, automation, integration, and transformation. When you move to the world of AI, you're using data in a more unfettered way than ever before. Therefore, getting data more pristine in our platforms becomes even more important going forward.

SL: Is what we see with AI revolutionary, or is it more of an evolutionary step in technology innovation?

LQ: It's a pretty significant evolutionary step as opposed to a revolutionary step. Why do I split hairs? It's evolutionary because research on machine learning and models has been heading this way for decades. The underlying computing capabilities have been under development for a very long time. But the advent of generative AI burst onto the world

71

stage in spectacular fashion. Technology's ability to create things that didn't exist was a watershed moment. We shouldn't underestimate the ability to say, "I'll describe an image, and have you display it," or "I want you to write this content for me." It's significant.

SL: I get the sense that you're about to add a qualifier here.

LQ: People do tend to overestimate what this will do in the short term. Some think we'll wake up one day and AI will be taking over the world. They'll be walking down Main Street and see AI-powered dinosaurs towering over the city and those kinds of things. AI will make us significantly more productive and will make their lives better. But will we wake up 10 years from now and be unable to recognize human existence or the human way of life? Absolutely not. That's not going to change that dramatically.

SL: CIOs constantly think about how they can help their businesses. What advice would you give to someone tasked with digital transformation in their organization about orchestrating integration and automation?

LQ: I would advise always thinking about the three "Ps" – people, process, and platforms. By far, the biggest "P" of all is people. Any transformation is about people. What will they get from this, and how can I prove they're getting it? Did we ask them if they liked it? Without that, I think we flounder. It sounds hokey, but can I make people happy with this? Can I make them smile? Can I make them think, "Wow, I don't know how you did this, but it works so much better."

Summary

What I love about this conversation with Larry is his emphasis on the human side of digital transformation. He reminds us that it's not just about implementing new technologies but about making life easier for the people who use them. Larry's insights underscore the importance of integration and automation as essential components of successful digital transformation. He also highlights how CIOs must adapt to a new reality where their role is no longer just about managing technology but about collaborating with business units to ensure technology truly serves the organization's needs. Larry also brings a balanced perspective to the AI revolution, recognizing its potential to enhance productivity while cautioning against overestimating its immediate impact. Ultimately, his focus on people, processes, and platforms provides a clear and practical framework for navigating the complexities of modern IT leadership.

Chapter 3

Data Management: The Perils of Disconnected Data

What we discuss in this chapter:

- Disconnected data is an unintended consequence of digital transformation, fueled by the explosion of applications, clouds, APIs, and other data sources.

- Without proper connectivity, data becomes just noise – useless sand in the gears of progress. Ensuring that trusted data is accessible has become more essential than ever because it's the fuel that powers AI engines.

- The North Carolina Department of Health and Human Services exemplifies how data can improve people's lives.

"Data is knowledge. Data is power."

At the onset of the global pandemic in 2020, as the magnitude of the crisis grew, no one could say with certainty what would happen next. In those dark days, it fell to public health agencies to guide an anxious public desperate for answers.

But that could only happen if the agencies had access to trusted, accurate, and timely data. Therefore, the role of government sector IT professionals suddenly became critical.

"We didn't know what each day would bring," said Babita Savitsky, Director of Technology and Architecture for the North Carolina Department of Health and Human Services.[35] "Things were changing every day. We were all scrambling."

The North Carolina Department of Health and Human Services (NCDHHS) manages services for the state's nearly 11 million citizens – especially the most vulnerable, such as children, seniors, people with physical challenges, and low-income families. That mission shifted into overdrive as the pandemic worsened. The IT team had to consolidate and transform raw data from disconnected sources to provide real-time insights to the state's leaders, so they could quickly make decisions that would have a direct impact on the public.

As NCDHHS did not have an enterprise-grade integration solution in place, IT struggled to keep up with the rapidly evolving situation. For instance, it could take up to 70 employee hours to update a single dashboard view, such as the availability of Personal Protective Equipment (PPE) – vital information for frontline workers.

"Our team was working 15–18-hour days and through weekends," Savitsky said. "We would call 2 a.m. 'party time' because that's when the data had to come together so it would be available to the public at 8 a.m. Bringing in data was a completely manual process. Then, we had to standardize it before we handed it to the analysts so they could do their work. There were no automated pipelines, so we had to manually update data, sometimes on an hourly basis. We had to provide the right data for the right people to make the right decisions."

Lives depended on it.

The IT team needed to integrate disparate systems, including the state's central on-premises data center, various state and federal health databases, and external partners. Also, automated pipelines were required to securely transport HIPAA-compliant structured and unstructured data to populate easy-to-understand dashboards for policymakers, the media, and the public. Savitsky consulted with the state's central IT office, the North Carolina Department of Information Technology, and found it had already purchased an AI-driven integration and automation platform for a massive, long-term project still in development.

The platform had the capabilities she required, including scalability, low-code/no-code functionality to allow her team to connect endpoints quickly, and reusability of processes so that team members didn't have to build integrations from scratch repeatedly.

Savitsky built her first integration in just 48 hours, and in less than a week, she had created a half-dozen data pipelines. ("I was living the dream, using out-of-the-box connectors," Savitsky said.) Then, the IT team began to pick up steam. The platform's efficiency resulted in 250-plus integrations and connecting with 30 endpoints during the first two years of the pandemic. They supported 21 dashboards that often were updated on an hourly basis. The public-facing dashboards received about 25 million views in 2021 alone.

Based on the data provided to department experts for analysis, North Carolina's governor and other top state leaders could make informed decisions on how best to deal with the fast-moving crisis. Citizens and frontline workers could see:

- Vaccination numbers for the state population
- Hospitalization rate for people with the virus
- Number of open beds in hospital ICUs
- Availability of PPE, such as masks, gloves, and face shields
- Vaccination numbers among seniors living in facilities, as well as for foster kids and the homeless

Dr. Mandy K. Cohen, the state's top health official, held almost daily press briefings that became must-see TV. She presented dashboards of vital information sourced from the NCDHHS IT team's data work. Many parents could return to work because a public dashboard showed which of the state's about 6,000 licensed daycares had openings for children. The data was so precise that officials could ensure vaccine availability in minority populations, which was a significant national problem.

Bloomberg News singled out North Carolina for being among the best-performing US states in distributing vaccines equitably. "That's partly because the state is by far the best at collecting demographic data," Bloomberg wrote.[36] Cohen, who later became the director of the Centers for Disease Control and Prevention, was widely praised for her leadership and the agency's focus on equity, data account-ability, and transparent communication. The team's efforts were also recognized in a national competition with a "State IT Innovation Award."[37]

Post-pandemic, the NCDHHS has continued to find other ways to leverage those new integration and data speed capabilities to deliver life-changing services.

System connectivity and data access have made large-scale managed care reporting immeasurably easier. Additionally, North Carolina has pioneered an innovative "whole person health" pro-gram called NCCARE360. This collaborative solution offers a coor-dinated, community-focused, and people-centered approach to delivering care and ensures everyone receives all their entitled social services and resources. This unique approach improves lives and decreases long-term healthcare costs at the state level.

"Actionable data in a timely manner can have a very big impact on people," Savitsky said. "Data is knowledge. Data is power."

It's the nature of IT teams to be laser-focused on the tasks in front of them. Savitsky said they don't take time to "smell the roses" and instead quickly move on to the next project. But over the past few years, her team has gained a greater appreciation of the impact of their work and the outcomes they enable. "It's about how many lives we've touched and the kind of service we provide," she said. "It makes you realize that the work we do makes a difference."

Key Points

- **Goal:** Eliminate disconnected systems and inefficient manual processes to provide rapid data access by integrating disparate sources and ensure the state's leaders and citizens always have access to essential information that helps keep everyone safe during the pandemic.

- **Human Impact:** The low-code development functionality of the AI-driven integration and automation platform reduced manual effort by 50–60%. In addition to the millions of North Carolina citizens accessing public dashboards during the pandemic, 350 key stakeholders used internal dashboards daily to help guide decision-making. Building off that success, the IT team uses faster data access to help people in other ways, including Medicaid/managed care and the nation's first statewide health services coordination platform.

- **Lessons Learned:** "What we did with the platform during the crisis was mind-blowing. But it's also about the people who can use the technology. In my mind, it's always people, process, and technology. Yes, there's a tool, and what it's delivering to us is amazing. But how we're able to use it is the key thing. Usually, it's the people creating the processes that make the difference. That's certainly true for us." – *Babita Savitsky, Director of Technology and Architecture, North Carolina Department of Health and Human Services*

The Challenge of Data Management

I grew up in North Carolina and still have family there, so this story warms my heart. It's a great example of the government harnessing data to protect citizens' interests.

Whenever a crisis strikes, there's always an urgent need to make sense of available data and get those insights into the hands of the right people so they can make the best possible decisions. The North Carolina Department of Health and Human Services recognized the scope of the pandemic early and quickly responded with the help of trusted data. Equally impressive is how the agency has used what it learned during the crisis to achieve other public health goals since then.

New challenges are always on the horizon. This is why the availability of accurate, real-time data is always a business priority. However, data management is a persistent problem businesses have been trying to solve for decades. There's one hard truth: Disconnected data is useless. It doesn't matter how much data you have if it's inaccessible. Without that, you're just pushing around sand – an endless task with no real value.

If the data you're analyzing is of poor quality, incomplete, or outdated, how can you have confidence about any conclusions it's based upon? Yet, if we're honest, most businesses have never managed their data well. The result is a common question within organizations: *Can we trust our data?*

Alas, probably not. It's primarily due to fragmented architectures – an unintended consequence of digital transformation. Disconnected systems lead to disconnected data. The explosion of new technologies and applications has created enormous amounts of data trapped in disparate systems, forming data silos. It's difficult to access, let alone synchronize. There are multiple copies of it in multiple places. Data may be updated in one system but not in another. Or it's "dark data," meaning you can't use it meaningfully because you don't know what it is or even where it is.

When analyzing a situation, we often think, "Well, the data is the data." This is true, except if your data is suspect. Then, being a data-driven organization is impossible.

This is why connecting systems is at the heart of building a solid data foundation. It's ground zero for data management. No business will ever get its data "perfect." It's a pipe dream. But there's no reason you can't improve data quality by taming architectural complexity.

I think about data management in terms of "The Four Vs" of data analytics: *volume, velocity, variety*, and *veracity*. A Gartner analyst named Doug Laney popularized the first three in 2001. Over time, the fourth, *veracity*, was added.[38]

- **Volume:** The vast amount of data generated from various sources has grown exponentially with application and data sprawl. It's compounded the already steep challenge of aggregating, synchronizing, processing, and analyzing large datasets efficiently.

- **Velocity:** This is how quickly a business generates, moves, and analyzes data. Transforming data to enable real-time decision-making has never been more critical.

- **Variety:** Here, we consider the different types of data. Is it structured, unstructured, or semi-structured? They require different tools for proper movement and processing.

- **Veracity:** This refers to the reliability of the data. High-quality data is clean, well-understood, and trustworthy, enabling businesses to make good decisions.

While these capture the core elements of data management, I humbly suggest a fifth "V" – *value*. There are formulas for calculating data value, but I'm unaware of any accepted standard, as value differs much like beauty in the eye of the beholder. Even if there were a benchmark, every business would ultimately determine the value of their data for themselves. But something we can all agree upon is that unavailable data has no value.

There's something else you should know about me: I'm not a student of the school that says all data is valuable. Far from it.

Data Is the New Sand

The Economist once published a landmark cover story proclaiming that data had replaced oil as the world's most valuable resource.[39] In my opinion, "data is the new oil" was always a simplistic and flawed concept. Yes, both are valuable raw materials that require processing. But the comparison falls apart in terms of supply. Oil is finite, while data can be infinite. So, let me offer a different analogy: Data is like sand.

Once, businesses were starving for information, scouring every corner for data to drive decision-making. But now, in the digital age, we're drowning in data. The real issue? Most of it is disconnected and practically useless. You end up sifting through endless grains of sand when very little of it is worth your time. We collect it, measure it, move it, and hoard it. But in all this frenzy, we lose sight of the fact that most of it isn't helpful.

We've fallen into the trap of thinking all data is valuable, which is the wrong approach. This creates a vast, Sahara-like expanse with endless dunes of information. Finding the useful bits is like searching for a needle in a haystack – or, in my analogy, a valuable diamond in all that sand. The sheer volume turns into a massive signal-noise problem, which is why data management has become such a cautionary tale for most businesses. The real question we need to ask ourselves is: How much of this data is helping us run our businesses?

Data sprawl is real. But it's more than just the applications and systems producing an overload of data. The different forms of data you're trying to wrangle within your business also contribute to the problem.

- **Structured Data:** Organized and formatted, structured data is easily searchable and processed. It includes information in spreadsheets, databases, and comma-separated values (CSV) files, such as numbers, dates, and categories.
- **Unstructured Data:** Unstructured data lacks organization and doesn't fit into traditional databases or tables. It can include text documents, images, video and audio files, and emails.
- **Semi-structured Data:** This data is a mix of structured and unstructured and contains a basic level of organization to make it more searchable. It can include XML and JSON files.

Here's one real-world example of an everyday data management problem. Who are the worst data entry people in the world? Salespeople! (Sales folks, I love you. But you know it's true.) Yet, they oversee inputting critical data about customers and prospects into your CRM – a crucial system of record. It will never be a priority for salespeople to enter the correct information in the proper fields because they're busy closing deals. So, what happens? Everyone does their own thing. That's why you might have five versions of "General Electric" in your CRM instead of everything under one company. On top of that, when you connect the CRM to an ERP system like NetSuite, the fields are different, the definitions of "customers" are different, and so on.

You've just teed yourself up for a big data management problem.

It's too easy today for businesses to stash data in repositories in the faint hope that, somehow, someone will leverage it for something.

Don't get me wrong: Data repositories are essential. Companies in that category are staking a claim for being indispensable in the age of AI. But it's also likely that most of the data you amass there is digital sand that won't ever help your business. It can even gum up your operational gears because pulling worthwhile insights from all that data takes much more time and effort.

There's no gold star for the business with the most data. But the most *useful* data is different.

My friend Matt McLarty, whom you'll read more about in an upcoming chapter about API management, has a thoughtful way of thinking about data. He and Stephen Fishman wrote about the economics of data in their recent book, *Unbundling the Enterprise.*[40] Let's just say that they are also not fans of the "data is the new oil" concept.

Matt notes that consolidating and centralizing data for analysis is vital work from a data science perspective. But even more critical is decentralizing and moving it as precise, contextualized, and actionable data. He believes that if data truly is the new currency for businesses, it only has value when liquid – not in terms of oil, but rather like financial asset liquidity. That's when businesses can spend it, especially when it comes to AI.

This requires a different kind of optimization. Data has no tangible value until it's consumed and put into action. Otherwise, it's just sitting in a lake, warehouse, etc., becoming a storage cost on the ledger sheet. This problem is common for organizations. But when you make precise slices of accurate data actionable for specific functions, then it becomes an asset.

Matt and I make the same point, although using slightly different language. Like all things in life, there needs to be a balance when it comes to data. Yes, data is an asset. Too much data, though, can be a liability. Data hoarding can even be prohibitively expensive for a business since data lake space isn't free. However, using the right data in the right amounts can be incredibly valuable. This is why thinking about data in terms of liquidity will be essential in the age of AI.

You shouldn't just amass vast amounts of data without understanding what it is or having a plan for its use. This is a very supply-side view of data where the focus is just dumping everything you can get your hands on into one central place. Instead, businesses need a demand-side view where the thought process is around how best to use your valuable data. A connectivity platform can break down those data silos and ensure that raw information flows freely for transformation into knowledge. But it's important to remember that AI requires clean, accurate, and trusted data.

Data connectivity is like that old saying: *With great power comes great responsibility.* You need a thoughtful data integration strategy to extract the best insights before employing technology to achieve that goal.

The Fuel That Drives AI

Much of the focus on AI today centers upon innovation with large language models. This is why, ultimately, business success will be determined by data in two different ways. First, publicly available and licensed data trains those models. Then, there's your proprietary data that augments and contextualizes the AI model for your specific purposes.

Right now, the importance of data is understated. A 2024 report by Constellation Research that surveyed more than 1,000 senior executives discovered that 77% believe AI will give them a competitive advantage and that 75% of respondents said they expect the technology to impact their roles significantly in the next three years.[41] It's great that businesses recognize the potential. But despite that high level of confidence in AI's impact on their companies, they still have

Data Management: The Perils of Disconnected Data

a significant data gap that needs addressing, according to R. "Ray" Wang, Constellation's Principal Analyst and Founder.

"This is why the first thing you need to do is get the data house in order," Ray says. "Companies are sitting on hundreds of applications that aren't connected. They just don't know where their data is."

And let's be real. They likely don't have a clear sense of how trustworthy that data is either. Ray sees data accuracy on a sliding scale, depending on the industry. For example, as he wrote in the foreword of this book, an 85% accuracy rate might be acceptable in customer support – maybe even worthy of a promotion. But in finance? That's a pink slip waiting to happen. And in health care? We don't even want to think about the consequences of that level of error! Ray's point is sharp. Access to accurate data is everything, especially when it comes to AI models that will drive mission-critical functions where mistakes aren't an option.

Now, let's bring this closer to home with something we all deal with – getting what we ordered at a fast-food drive-thru.

For the record, I have a soft spot for spicy chicken nuggets and chili from a popular chain with a logo that features a red-haired girl with pigtails. (Judge me if you want, but that chili hits the spot!) We've all been there, ordering through a menu board speaker system. You inch forward, place your order, drive to the window, pay, and get your meal – only to find out you've got the wrong drink or are missing your onion rings. Frustrating, right?

This is where AI comes into play. I'm certain AI will be taking our drive-thru orders within the next two years. In fact, not long after I first wrote this, my favorite fast-food chain announced it's already experimenting with AI-driven ordering. Other chains are doing the same, testing how AI could improve these experiences.

But before AI can make our fast-food runs seamless, these restaurants will need vast amounts of the right data to train their models to process orders accurately, like: "I want a burger with fries, but hold the pickles and give me extra ketchup." The AI will need to understand different voices, dialects, and accents – not to mention the variety of burger toppings. The volume of data required to train these models will be staggering because, let's face it, when you're craving your favorite meal, 85% accuracy just won't cut it.

The bottom line? AI is coming to a drive-thru near you. It's going to happen because AI will be more accurate, and the food will be ready faster. But a data problem will need to be solved first. This is how every business should think about AI – do you have the accurate data needed to effectively deliver products and services to your customers?

Thomas H. Davenport is a prolific author, professor, and business advisor. He has written or edited more than 20 books, specializing in analytics and AI. When Tom talks about data, people listen. He minces no words about the importance of data in AI.

"I think data is the primary competitive advantage in the AI world," Tom said while onstage at an event in late 2023. "But AI can only fuel a company if data first fuels AI. Companies serious about AI must be serious about data – collecting, integrating, storing, and making it broadly accessible. None of these is a new challenge, but it is even more important now if an organization cares about AI. It's not hard to analyze data anymore. What's hard is having your data in good condition in the first place."

Tom's recent book, *All in on AI*, co-written with Nitin Mittal, a principal with Deloitte Consulting, explains how accurate predictions aren't possible without vast quantities of good data. They highlight the importance of data integration.

"Every organization that's serious about AI must deal with its data at some point – structuring or rearchitecting it, putting it on a common platform, and addressing pesky issues such as data quality, duplicated data, and siloed data throughout the company," the authors wrote. "It's fair to say that the single biggest obstacle for most organizations in scaling AI systems is acquiring, cleaning, and integrating the right data."[42]

An AI strategy is a data strategy, bringing us back to the need for connection.

Connectivity in an AI Data Management Strategy

In nearly three decades of business, I've seen one constant flaw in data management: the overlooked importance of how information flows across an organization. Mishandling data transport is a critical reason why digital transformation, cloud migration, and data warehouse projects often fail. Whether it's integration, automation, API management, ETL, ELT, iPaaS, or another flow method, they all boil down to one thing: moving data. And I'll keep hammering home this simple truth: Disconnected data is useless data. Without seamless connectivity, your data is just a pile of numbers, powerless to drive tangible business outcomes – especially in an AI-driven world.

The availability of accurate, trusted, and timely data is the North Star for every enterprise. Yet businesses often assume that data connectivity will happen magically – until they realize it doesn't. Then, it's sheer panic. However, a unified layer of connectivity rectifies the issue by ensuring seamless data movement to both internal foundational systems and external-facing applications. This isn't just about improving efficiency. It's about ensuring your data can do something. Without integration, disconnected data is a dead end (Figure 3.1).

Here are some points to consider when creating the connectivity tissue for your business to get the most from data and prepare for AI.

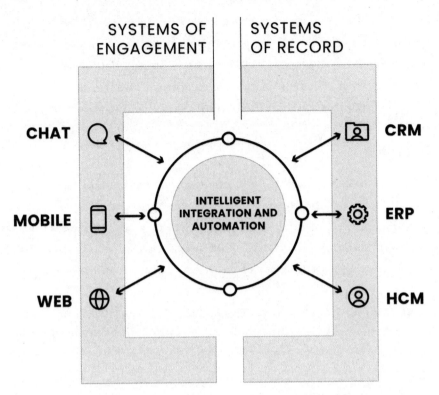

Figure 3.1 The value of intelligent integration and automation.

Single Platform

Simplicity matters. A unified integration tool to connect every system reduces complexity instead of adding to it. It provides one-stop shopping for everything integration and automation. Connecting foundational systems, applications, databases, clouds, and other endpoints ensures everything talks to each other. Breaking down silos solves problems of incomplete, unsynchronized, and unknown data while ensuring data always gets where it's needed.

It also helps mitigate risks. The darker side of a fragmented IT infrastructure is that bad actors can more easily access your data. A unified integration layer consolidates your security efforts by drastically reducing the risk plane and providing greater visibility.

Data Management: The Perils of Disconnected Data

I know it's difficult to get to a single platform given the four Vs of data. But I see the other side of this argument all too often, where companies have five, ten, or even twenty different data management and integration products/platforms. All you've done in this instance is layer a data management nightmare on top of a data nightmare.

Data Hub

A data repository creates "golden records" as a single source of truth throughout the business. It eliminates the problem of unsynchronized data and enables businesses to develop trusted records with agreed-upon standards. For instance, you won't have six regions across North America with six different definitions of a closed sale.

A data hub acts as a brain. It takes data from systems, standardizes it, and sends back the correct information to all appropriate applications. For example, if a customer's address changes in the ERP, a data hub will ensure those changes are automatically made in the CRM and any other needed system. High-quality data is always curated and synchronized across platforms around customers, employees, partners, and more.

Large Data Movement

As data becomes more critical in the age of AI, the role of storage sites is growing, whether they are data lakes (raw data), data warehouses (processed data), or data marts (data for specific business units).

Moving massive amounts of data in and out of these repositories in bulk transfers at low latency requires heavy-duty ELT or ETL capabilities. It's also not just about the volume of data but the frequency of bulk data transfers.

Real-Time Data Access

In a world where transactions happen in fractions of a second, the definition of what qualifies as "outdated" data is getting shorter. Real-time data access has become critical for delivering the customer experiences people expect and ensuring businesses have the timeliest insights for decision-making.

Connectivity that automates accessibility to multiple data sources and workflow processes can lessen the possibility of mistakes that undermine customer relationships or lead the business to make faulty decisions based on data that has passed its expiration date.

AI-Readiness

Every company is a data company, regardless of size or industry. When it comes to construction, you probably think of steel and concrete. But Boston-based Suffolk Construction considers data the foundation of everything it builds. I encourage you to visit the company's website because the scope of its work is visionary.[43]

Dinesh Singh, Suffolk Construction's Director of Enterprise Development and Architecture, said the Boomi Enterprise Platform's DataHub capability processes, dedupes, and cleans the equivalent of nearly 120,000 volumes of Harry Potter books every single day. That's 1,500 processes daily with 30 connected applications around financials, safety, and more.

"Our business decision-making depends upon this," Singh said. "Our safety depends upon this. Our future use cases depend on this. Boomi provides absolute reliability."

The platform has also laid the groundwork for pilot projects experimenting with AI. One is analyzing worksite safety data and creating "tripwire" metrics to better predict and prevent incidents. Another safety initiative involves integrating camera data to determine which areas at job sites are especially hazardous. Singh said providing AI with the right data is crucial for those projects. This means ensuring the integrity of the data by keeping the pipelines between systems connected. In fact, Singh suggests that every business needs to think like this regarding AI initiatives.

"It's not time to sit tight," Singh added. "I sometimes hear people saying, 'Sit, wait, have a deep breath.' Don't do that! You have so much homework to do right now, so get to that. If you're not ready with the integration architecture, you will be in trouble because AI will come whether or not you're ready. If you don't have clean data, you'll have problems. You need to clean up your data before you can use AI. Once you integrate clean data with AI, you can do anything."

With that advice in mind, here's a high-level checklist for preparing your data for AI:

- **Consolidation:** Aggregate data from every available source to ensure AI models have the best, most comprehensive datasets to learn from – improving accuracy.

- **Quality:** Synchronize, standardize, and clean data to reduce the problem of bad data that can lead to inaccurate AI models.

- **Timeliness:** Real-time data access allows businesses to quickly adapt to changing circumstances and address issues before they become full-blown problems.

- **Automation:** Automate data pipelines to curtail the risk of human error and speed up workflows.

- **Governance:** Manage data risk to establish accountability for both internal standards and regulatory compliance.

- **Security and Privacy:** Secure data from breaches to instill confidence and trust that personally identifiable information is handled responsibly.

- **Grounding:** Enhance data quality with proprietary information to provide greater context and accuracy, such as through retrieval-augmented generation (RAG).

- **Storage and Management:** Enable smooth transport of large volumes of data in and out of storage systems such as lakes and warehouses.

- **Visibility:** Create a 360-degree view of data to monitor the performance of AI models over time to ensure reliability.

Integration is a vital part of a broader data strategy. It comes back to those Vs – *volume, velocity, variety, veracity*, and my addition, *value*. The basics of data management help you to tame data sprawl, improve quality and accuracy, and ensure it's always available to those who need it. The bonus is that it goes a long way toward making your enterprise AI-ready.

If you can't articulate that kind of clear data strategy, then all you're doing is pushing sand from one place to another. And that's a great lead-in to my conversation with a genuine giant of business, Mark Fields.

Chapter Takeaway

Three Things to Know

1. It's common for businesses to lack visibility into their data because applications, databases, and clouds aren't fully integrated and automated.
2. Focusing on a connected data foundation is the best way to ensure that AI doesn't become just another shiny object in your digital infrastructure.

(continued)

Data Management: The Perils of Disconnected Data

(continued)

3. Getting your data house in order must be a priority because if you don't fill the gaps in your data access today, you won't be able to train your AI models properly on your business.

Why It Matters

Delivering business value in the age of AI requires trusted data. Sometimes, you need less data than you think because vast amounts of information that serve no discernable purpose produce no value.

The Bottom Line

Providing access to the right data at the right time for the right people has always been essential. However, harnessing the value of data will be the difference between success and failure as you try to unlock AI's potential.

A Conversation with Mark Fields

■ ■ ■

Mark Fields is a transformative business leader of multibillion-dollar companies. At 38, he was the youngest-ever head of a major Japanese company when he became president and CEO of the Mazda Motor Corporation in 2000. But he's best known for his leadership at one of the most iconic brands the world has ever known: the Ford Motor Company.

As CEO, Mark moved Ford into the future by delivering innovation, transformation, and growth during a time of great uncertainty throughout the automotive industry. He revitalized Ford with the introduction of electric vehicles while also returning to its past with the debut of the latest version of the legendary Ford GT Super Car.

His "Way Forward" plan made the company's North American operations leaner and more productive. He also earned a reputation for improving cross-functional communication and reducing team friction across the huge organization. Few companies rival Ford's size, complexity, and size, and Mark is one of the few people on the planet qualified to run a manufacturing giant of that scale.

Mark also served as the interim CEO of Hertz. Today, he's a senior advisor to TPG Capital and sits on the corporate boards of several companies. On a personal level, Mark and I just love talking about automobiles. It should come as no surprise that Mark is a passionate, American-made muscle-car guy. He's also an all-around badass.

Steve Lucas: Every business has been thinking about digital transformation for years. Now, the growing impact of AI has been added to the mix. From a senior leadership perspective, how do you view AI, and what do you see coming?

Mark Fields: How I wish we had AI when I ran Ford. Like many companies, we suffered from working in silos. You had the European organization, the North American organization, the Pacific organization, product development, parts and service, etc. Creating a common data lake and pulling all that good data on customers, dealers, and vehicle service would have allowed us to do some interesting things with that information using AI. We could make more tailored offers to consumers based on what they own now, how long they've had those vehicles, and their service history. There's an old saying: *50% of the advertising is effective; the other 50% is not. You just don't know which one is.* I wish we could have linked that kind of information together and made better use of our advertising budget. Another example where AI would help is closing the information gap between our warranty and service teams and the manufacturing side. We could have had early warning systems from warranty data in the field right back into the manufacturing organization. That would have helped the purchasing organization too. Let's say we were seeing early signs of a sensor failure. We could have gone back to the manufacturer of that sensor and said, "We're detecting that this is going to be a problem. How do we get ahead of it?"

SL: So, you see digital transformation and AI going hand in hand?

MF: When we started on digital transformation at Ford, I created a single data and analytics group. We found that we had pockets of the company doing various versions of data analytics. But it was only on their data. There were huge opportunities for, say, the product development organization to share their data with the manufacturing group early on. So, if the engineers had this great new idea for an engine, transmission, or HVAC system, the manufacturing folks could say, "Hold on, if you design it that way, it will cost more, and servicing it will be harder." AI can give you that kind of information. I'll also say that it's great to have data and analytics, but it's another thing to make sure that our people are asking the right questions. AI does that because you don't even have to ask the questions. It will actually prompt you. In my day at Ford, I saw all this data. But it took a long time to extract insights. That meant we often had to redo work, which led to additional costs and timing implications. AI can tell a program manager, "Based on the latest information, you're going to run into a wall in Week 36 with this problem, and here are five things you can do about that now." I see AI, for lack of a better term, as being a co-pilot. That's priceless.

SL: I hear you saying that AI can instantly provide the context for businesses that might typically only come through decades of learning, pain, and experience. You know, the gray hair philosophy.

MF: Correct. With the aid of AI, you improve speed, efficiency, productivity, and effectiveness throughout the organization based on having the data and being able to link it. Then, having an AI layer on top of it all to extract insights is pretty transformational.

SL: The first place you went with AI is the importance of having all your data in one place and making sure it's accessible. Otherwise, it's not practical for AI.

MF: Absolutely. Let's use car manufacturing as an example. There's tremendous cost, time, and effort when you design a vehicle. You build your first series of prototypes and then probably another series of four or five pre production builds before you ever get to job one. There's tremendous engineering expense. In a business like the auto industry, which is interconnected between product development, manufacturing, warrant, purchasing, etc., the value comes with having the data, linking it to everyone, and then having an AI overlay. Nirvana in the auto industry is reducing that time because it translates to effort and expense. AI creates huge amounts of efficiencies there.

SL: How about AI's role in creating new car designs?

MF: It used to be that as soon as you walked through the door of the design center, there was a strong smell of clay. That's because everything had to be modeled. Now, you walk into a design center, put on a VR set, and look at designs in 3D. AI is absolutely getting us to the point of putting those images in a buildable digital format. It gets back to my point that the companies that will win are the ones most efficient in the concept-to-customer piece.

SL: Anything else that pops into your head as a significant impact area for AI?

MF: Purchasing. When I was at Ford Motor Company, we purchased $90 billion of annual billable materials from suppliers. How do you monitor quality coming from your suppliers when a vehicle, on average, has 4,000 parts? That's a huge opportunity for AI. Another crucial area is understanding the financial health of the suppliers because if they have problems, the whole supply chain is at risk. Think about how AI can make it so easy that you could get a complete dashboard of their health from a financial viability standpoint.

SL: Could you see an AI agent, rather than a dashboard, that continually monitors the health of these suppliers? I create an agent that taps into public financial data, news feeds, etc., and then tell it to watch this company and alert me if something is troubling.

MF: Absolutely. Every automaker is always trying to de-risk their supply chain. In my time, I never had a tier-one supplier ever shut us down. It was always the tier-two and tier-three suppliers that shut us down because we didn't have good visibility down there and never saw it coming. That's where an AI agent that could flag those things early would be hugely valuable.

SL: Here's a question I know is on many minds. Do you think that AI takes jobs from people?

MF: When you think about AI these days, one of the things everybody's very scared of is universal job displacement. I don't subscribe to that. Historically, there has been some job displacement with innovation, whether it was steam, which led to electricity, which led to machinery, and which led to cyber systems. There will always be some kind of dislocation for a period of time. But then more of other jobs will be created. Maybe there will be some reduction in the headcount in some areas, but also reallocation to different needs that aren't being met. One of the big benefits of AI is operational efficiency improvements. At the same time, whenever somebody wants a new initiative in any company and in any function, they also say, "And oh, by the way, we need 10 more people to fund it."

SL: You know how I love cars. How do you think AI will impact the consumer's driving experience?

A Conversation with Mark Fields

MF: The biggest change in consumer experience within the vehicle will be the advent of a voice-activated virtual system. We were working toward that at Ford, but every time we tried to add a new feature to the architecture, it looked like a spaghetti junction. The biggest transformation will be how people interact with their cars. For example, you literally will be having a conversation with your car, saying, "Hey, I'm really hungry. Can you find the nearest Dunkin' Donuts, program that into the GPS, and get me there?" Or you're listening to the radio, and you hear Pink on the radio, and your spouse loves Pink. And you say, "Can you find out when Pink is playing in our area, and if tickets are available, can I buy two?" Today, there's a whole issue with driver distraction, touch screens, and other kinds of stuff. The easiest way humans can interact with their vehicles safely is the same way they interact with other humans in the car. AI is going to make that happen.

SL: Why do you think connecting and integrating systems is so important?

MF: Every industry is a technology industry. I don't care whether you're selling tomatoes or building cars. Technology and enabling technologies in your products are going to be ubiquitous. Everything's a node in the future. One of the biggest challenges in the auto industry is integrating systems. Integrating an infotainment system from a supplier into the electrical architecture and making sure that it's hermetically sealed from the mission-critical systems is really, really hard. I don't care if it's consumer electronic items, airplanes, or business systems. Integration helping AI is going to be a huge enabler.

SL: Do you think CEOs care enough about their integration and automation strategy, or do they just leave it for their CIOs and IT teams to figure it out?

MF: CEOs come at it from the lens of, "How do I continue to accelerate growth, improve margins, improve customer satisfaction, improve quality, and create shareholder value?" Then, they start getting down to what the enablers are for all of that. I don't think the first thoughts that pop up in their head in the morning are integration and automation. But the best CEOs ask questions like, "For us to achieve these things, what's necessary to get there?" That's where those strategies are uncovered.

SL: Are there any cautionary notes you think CEOs need to know about potential risk, safety, and other issues related to AI?

MF: When you and I were just starting our careers, we quickly became familiar with the saying, "Garbage in, garbage out."

SL: The same thing applies to AI.

MF: That's right. Every CEO needs to ask themselves, "Yeah, I understand AI. I understand the benefits. But do I have the right data that will give me the right insights for my business?" It would be a very clarifying question for a CEO to ask their CIO: "What's the status of our data?"

SL: So, is it safe to say you believe that every CEO's first question before starting their AI journey should be, "Do I have the right data?"

MF: Exactly.

Summary

What I love about this conversation with Mark Fields is his clear understanding of how AI can revolutionize industries – particularly the automotive sector, where he's spent much of his career. Mark's insights go beyond the technical. He emphasizes the real-world applications of AI, from improving cross-functional communication to creating early warning systems for manufacturing issues. He sees AI as a co-pilot, helping businesses avoid costly mistakes and improving efficiency across the board.

But what really stands out is his focus on the foundational element of all this innovation: data. He led with a growth mindset at Ford, and the fuel for that accelerated growth was data. Mark believes that before any company can harness the power of AI, it needs to ensure its data is accurate, connected, and accessible. His perspective is a crucial reminder that while AI offers incredible potential, its success hinges on a company's ability to manage and integrate data effectively.

Chapter 4

Automation: Creating Enterprise Efficiency

What we discuss in this chapter:

- The real power of connecting systems is in what it enables – the automation of workflows and processes.

- AI is taking automation to the next level by adding great adaptability, flexibility, and stability to automated workflows while adding the element of reasoning with autonomous agents.

- How Kalyra uses system integration and data automation to help make lives better for senior citizens.

"These are the things integration and automation allow us to provide."

When organizations think about metrics that show the value of any technology system for their business, they typically consider time and money saved, productivity gains, and other efficiencies. These are all vital considerations for not-for-profits too. However, another key performance indicator (KPI) is harder to fit on a spreadsheet: how technology helps improve lives.

Kalyra,[44] a South Australian organization that helps older people comfortably maintain independence with aged care services and living facilities, believes creating a better quality of life is the ultimate benchmark. This is how Kalyra measures the importance of a technology platform that connects its critical systems.

"Integrating and automating processes means we can focus more on those value-added services that our clients and our residents want," said Nicole Fishers, Kalyra's General Manager of Information and Digital Services. "If we're spending all our time doing duplicate data entry or having to do processing manually, we're not providing services for some of the most vulnerable people in our community."

Connected systems enable Kalyra to have and schedule the right staff to support and assist seniors. That allows people to stay in their homes longer, have access to affordable housing, and enjoy a greater sense of dignity in their golden years.

"These are the things that integration and automation allow us to provide," Fishers said.

Kalyra, which derives from an Aboriginal word that means "a pleasant or good place," has a storied history of helping people. Its genesis was the philanthropic James Brown Memorial Trust, which was founded in 1892 to serve the community. Over more than 130 years, Kalyra's work has included fighting polio and tuberculosis, and in recent decades, it has concentrated on aged care services.

Today, there are three primary pillars to that mission. One is "Help at Home" community care, which provides domestic assistance such as nursing care visits to seniors in their homes. Another is operating three Residential Aged Care facilities. The third is maintaining seven retirement living villages and affordable care housing for those at risk of homelessness. It's a broad portfolio of services that ensures the well-being of thousands of seniors. It also explains the guiding principle that is Kalyra's motto: "It's different here."

The organization is expanding fast to support an aging population and now has 600 employees. But with growth came stiff challenges around digital complexity, duplicative systems, and data quality. Previously, there had been no cohesive digital strategy as teams worked on an ad hoc basis. Critical data about clients and residents was repeatedly entered into multiple applications, leading to wasted effort and errors.

Fishers joined Kalyra in 2023 to initiate a digital transformation that included breaking down those silos. She knew that integration and automation would be at the heart of that strategy.

Previously, Fishers had used the Boomi Enterprise Platform to create a more connected campus at Flinders University,[45] a college with more than 25,000 students. At Kalyra, Fishers' team uses the platform to knit together critical systems and ensure the organization completely understands the needs of every senior. Applications for HR, finance, payroll, clinical management, home care scheduling, and more are no longer fragmented. They're part of a unified digital architecture. The platform's DataHub capabilities enable a trusted "golden record" for each person. That way, their consistent data can be automatically shared throughout every system, eliminating manual data entry and reducing mistakes that negatively impact care.

Connectivity also contributes to several other key areas. For instance, it powers an app that provides residents, clients, and family members easy access to information about services. It's also vastly improved the onboarding and offboarding processes for employees. The frontline workforce for elder care can be transient, with up to 40% turnover annually. So, getting new staff up and running fast is vital. Connectivity will also enable Kalyra to integrate directly with government systems to meet regulatory reporting requirements.

The integration and automation platform will be central to several large transformation initiatives on the Kalyra road map. These include implementing a new clinical management system, replacing the HR system, and perhaps the most challenging of all, determining the role of artificial intelligence. Fishers sees great potential for AI

Automation: Creating Enterprise Efficiency

in the aged care sector. However, she also emphasizes the need to consider the human element.

"I'm incredibly interested in the intersection between psychology and technology, AI, and robotics," she said. "We know this is an area where there's lots of opportunity for us to do some really amazing things to provide great quality of life. But one of the big issues is acceptance from elderly people in the use of those technologies. From a psychological perspective, we need to consider how to get that acceptance and usage from that cohort. That has to be part of any AI roadmap."

Key Points

- **Goal:** Maximize the effectiveness of digital systems by connecting critical applications and automating processes so staff can focus their time, energy, and efforts on what matters most – providing excellent services for the elderly population.

- **Human Impact:** The tangible effect of connected systems is how they directly affect seniors. Proper staffing is available in aged care facilities and community care teams. Seniors and their families have instant access to information about resources, services, and their financial statements via an app. (Kalyra is also exploring adding early-warning alert capabilities for natural disasters such as bushfires.) Perhaps most importantly, people always feel like care is personalized for them.

- **Lessons Learned:** "This goes back to the idea of KPIs. We were looking at an application software provider that might have saved our staff time through the reduction of calls from clients. But one of our regional managers noted that a lot of those clients live by themselves and may not have a lot of social interaction. They want to pick up the phone because that might be their weekly conversation with somebody. So, that interaction might be a good service we provided to a particular client. Efficiency isn't always the right measure for success. Asking, 'What is the value that we're adding?' is a better approach. Sometimes, choice is that value-add." – *Nicole Fishers, General Manager of Information and Digital Services, Kalyra*

Connection Enables Automation

Nicole Fishers gives us a lot to think about here. One is how data connection and automating workflows can operate behind the scenes, unseen, to directly impact people's health and care. Another is how she talks about integration and automation. Nicole doesn't necessarily think of them as something separate but rather how they go hand in hand.

She's not alone, either. I hear it a lot when I speak to technical leaders. Relatively early in my tenure as CEO of Boomi, I traveled to more than 20 countries and met with hundreds of business leaders to learn about their challenges in connecting systems and data. I was doing more listening than speaking.

I was in "absorb" mode. This is a technique I learned from Adobe CEO Shantanu Narayen.[46] Shantanu is among the world's best business leaders, and I was lucky to work closely with him after Adobe bought one of my previous companies, Marketo. It was fascinating to watch his management style up close. Shantanu tends not to make any decisions until he thoroughly understands the parameters. He will say that he's "absorbing." Like any CEO, he sometimes needs to act quickly. But he never rushes to any conclusion needlessly. It's only when satisfied that he's thoroughly analyzed all the available information that he acts. Usually, it's the right decision.

One of the things I absorbed during my first few months at Boomi is how businesses often think about an integration platform primarily as a means to an end. The real value is around what that connectivity can enable them to automate. Since I'm endlessly curious, I would always follow up with a question: "So, what does automation mean to you?"

The word I heard time and again was "process." Leaders would tell me that integration supports their business processes, allows them to build workflows, and helps in their understanding of the data. They see integration as the tool required to achieve their desired outcomes – not an outcome itself. Candidly, that was eye-opening for me. (It's another example of the importance of listening closely to what customers tell you.)

Automation allows organizations to be more agile, cost-effective, and innovative than market rivals. Every CIO is looking to achieve those things with their IT organization. They're not building integrations. They're creating processes to make their company more competitive.

This is why I'm fixated on the dual concepts of integration *and* automation. In the grand tradition of business buzzwords, other phrases get tossed around a lot today, like hyperautomation. I'll concede that does sound kind of cool. But as I've written already, I'm not a big fan of labels. What's important is to remember the basics. Businesses need to interconnect systems and build processes that run across them. That's just plain old integration and automation. They are two sides of the same coin. It's impossible to have one without the other. Together, they are a force multiplier. They go together like peanut butter and jelly.

Automation, in simple terms, reduces the need for constant human involvement, allowing employees to focus on more creative work. This shift minimizes errors, lowers security risks, and alleviates repetitive tasks. With AI, automation can evolve beyond predefined rules, introducing reasoning capabilities that further decrease the need for hands-on oversight.

And while you may think AI's role in automation is a decade away, the future is already here.

The Evolution of Automation

When it comes to historical markers for automation, my mind always goes back to Henry Ford and the automobile assembly line in the early 1900s. (Here I am with yet another car reference.) Ford disrupted the entire industry by building a more productive process that forever changed how people thought about manufacturing.

Ford didn't invent the assembly line. But he revolutionized the concept by taking a bespoke, complicated, and slow process and drastically reducing the time it took to mass-produce automobiles – cranking out millions of Model Ts. This made cars more affordable for the general public and probably did more to connect people than anyone of his time through expanding transportation.

His innovations around the division of labor with specialized tasks to get more from human talent, interchangeable parts, and continuous process flows laid the groundwork for how we think of modern automation in terms of computer systems. The goals are the same today.

- Efficiency
- Speed
- Cost savings

Ever since the dawn of digital systems, automation has existed. The first phrase I think of is "if, then, else." For me, the if–then–else statement marked the beginning of automation as we now think about it. This is the foundation of computer programming.

It automates your decision-making by allowing software to choose between actions depending on predetermined criteria. Whatever path a process takes is based on whether a specific condition is true or false.

For most of the digital era, if–then–else automation was custom or homegrown. Developers would write code from scratch to connect mainframes, PCs, Linux systems, etc. Or at least they would write the "last-mile" code for systems that weren't interoperable – even though the systems' makers claimed they were. (By the way, the irony of manually writing code to automate processes is not lost on me.) Because it was just code, that version of automation was considered "headless."

But how we think about business automation today is "headed." ERP and CRM vendors get the credit for starting it. Do we usually consider an ERP or CRM business an automation company? Not in the classic definition. But that's what they do. They manage the most critical systems in our businesses by automating processes around finance, sales, supply chain, and more.

It began with Hasso Plattner, who co-founded SAP in 1972.[47] (I remember that date because it was the same year I was born. I had the opportunity to work closely with Hasso on SAP HANA.) His brilliant idea was to recognize that none of the systems running businesses were automated. So, he and some like-minded colleagues started a company to automate finance, manufacturing processes, and more. Larry Ellison would do the same thing a few years later with Oracle.[48] They built applications with graphical interfaces that provided good user experiences on the front end while automating processes under the hood. It was an idea that Microsoft and Salesforce would champion too. When these industry giants were establishing themselves, they were sometimes referred to by a category term you don't hear as much now – business process automation.

The magic that the SAPs and Salesforces of the world tapped into was that they could automate all the processes within the four walls of their systems. SAP automated all the processes within SAP, and Salesforce automated all the processes within the Salesforce cloud. So, if you ran your business entirely in SAP, you solved the automation problem. But that's "intra" automation – happening within a single system.

No one was ready for the exploding application sprawl problem. As best-of-breed solutions became commonplace, IT needed interoperability, flexibility, and workflow automation between disparate applications. That required "inter" automation – happening between multiple systems. For instance, if someone was buying a product on your website, you needed a way for your hosting application to automatically notify your CRM system, your ERP system, supply chain partners, and so on.

Robotic process automation (RPA) emerged in the early 2000s. RPA could work across applications and automate actions that would have taken humans valuable time clicking away to process invoices and perform other rote tasks. It was quite clever. But it's also never been perfect. RPA is precisely what its name suggests – robotic. It does what it's told, period.

So today, we're in a hyper-saturated market overflowing with countless automation software solutions. I wouldn't even venture to guess at a number. They come in all shapes, forms, and flavors. But I want to make two points.

1. Automating processes between systems is a solvable problem.

2. Automating processes takes a lot of work.

Think about the complications. First, you must ensure that systems not designed to talk to one another can and will communicate. Then,

Automation: Creating Enterprise Efficiency

you have to rationalize the information between those systems. This could be something as simple as how dates get recorded. For example, the date format in one may be March 9, 2025, but in the other, it's 3/9/2025. Differences in definitions also need to be taken into account. Even the word "account" can mean different things in different systems.

But again, these are solvable challenges. I see examples of successful automation every day. This is why I believe it can change the trajectory of lives.

One is a large public university system with 450,000 students at 23 campuses. For many of those students, financial aid can make the difference between getting a life-changing education and not attending college at all. However, determining who might be eligible for a state grant was time-consuming and nerve-wracking for potential recipients. Processing applications could take a month and require 70 hours of manual work by financial aid teams. This was often time that students didn't have.

Enter AI-driven integration and automation. Leveraging the Boomi Enterprise Platform to connect data systems dramatically reduced the application-to-distribution time – now just three days. "For many students, this is the difference between enrolling and dropping out," said the university system's CIO.

This is the transformative power of automation.

Still, automating processes at scale requires tremendous effort and synchronization. One challenge is the inevitable changes that occur in the lifecycle of any process. You already know I believe in universal truths. Here's another one that explains the effort required to manage automated processes. Whenever something changes, the process typically breaks. Automations are brittle and require constant fixing because businesses are dynamic and always evolving.

Yes, we've made extraordinary progress in removing humans from significant portions of monotonous work to make our businesses more efficient. I would even suggest that we're almost at peak productivity in terms of how we've previously thought of automation. But we've hit a wall. A breakthrough is needed.

Fortunately, the AI revolution is here.

AI Meets Automation

AI is transforming automation by adding adaptability and reasoning, allowing it to make decisions and maintain processes independently. While AI still involves human oversight, it significantly reduces the need for hands-on involvement, particularly in data-intensive processes such as business intelligence and analytics. This shift is paving the way for algorithms to make complex decisions autonomously.

We're already seeing how AI optimizes processes that we now consider automated and uplevels them by powering self-service models for employees, customers, and partners. This includes improving supply chain efficiency, inventory management, logistics, shipping, procurement, auditing and fraud detection, compliance, talent acquisition, employee onboarding and offboarding, manufacturing quality control, and more. Every part of business will be impacted.

I could fill a chapter just with a long list of how automation and AI agents will make – and are making – work better and faster for employees and businesses. Instead, I'll mention a few common processes that traditionally have been somewhat automated but are now being super-automated with the help of AI. These are examples of practical applications that take advantage of an AI-driven integration and automation platform's capabilities.

Lead Response

Inside Sales teams are integral to most businesses today. Sales development reps (SDRs) represent the tip of the spear, making initial contact with prospects, determining whether those people are potential customers, and then passing qualified leads to account representatives for further conversations. I have nothing but respect for SDRs because they have a tough job that requires dealing with frequent rejection. SDRs need thick skin and must also be hard workers because there's always something to do.

Some sales development workflow processes are already automated today. Maybe a lead comes through my old marketing automation company, Marketo, and the SDR gets an alert when it's sent automatically to Salesforce. But from there, following up with the prospect has traditionally been a manual process. An SDR must do background research on the person, the company, and the industry. Then, they must write an email, craft a LinkedIn introduction, prepare a short phone call pitch, etc. It's very time intensive.

All of that is for just one lead.

A practical AI process drastically reduces the time required to handle each lead. When a lead drops into Salesforce, the AI-driven integration and automation platform automatically reaches out to an LLM – for instance, ChatGPT – submitting the prospect's name, title, and company name. It compiles research and writes a compelling email with the top three benefits of your company for the prospect's business. Those benefits come from proprietary information the platform feeds into your LLM through a process called retrieval-augmented generation (RAG) to provide greater context on why the person should care about your product or service.

A suggested email goes to the SDR, who can review and tweak it as needed. The SDR can use the time previously spent writing those emails to connect with more prospects. Meanwhile, the business significantly increases its capacity to address more leads faster.

Customer Service

In the last chapter, we briefly covered Constellation Research's R. "Ray" Wang's idea about the sliding scale of data accuracy. Ray noted that 85% trustworthy data is pretty good for customer support. In theory, this extends to an 85% rate of successfully resolving issues and keeping customers happy. Most business leaders would be very content with these numbers.

But achieving this kind of score is incredibly difficult. Customer and tech support jobs aren't a day at the beach, either. They're challenging roles, and the people in them are prone to burnout. They deal with frustrated customers who often demand their problems be solved immediately, which is stressful and exhausting.

Businesses have tried removing humans from the equation with chatbots and other self-help services. But if we're honest, the chatbots we've become familiar with often behave like "dumb bots," making customers more frustrated and more likely to yell louder at any live human representative that they (finally) get on the phone.

This is why customer support is so ripe for AI-infused automation. Like my example about AI at the fast-food drive-thru, AI's accuracy will be better. But the ability to reason is where AI-powered automation shines. Instead of dumb bots that have pre-programmed responses, chatbots will understand the context, enabling them to answer questions better and solve problems more conversationally, resolving a higher number of common issues faster. This will allow the humans in the customer support team to focus on the more complicated problems that really do require their expertise and knowledge.

Marketing Automation

Personalization is everything in marketing. You want to speak to people like individuals. But it's usually apparent when businesses really don't know the people they're trying to reach. Let's use the example of me buying a tent from an online company we all know. For the record, I can't stand camping. (For me, camping is anything where I don't have access to a hair dryer.) But I did buy a tent for my brother, who loves the outdoors. So, what happened after I hit the "purchase" button? You guessed it. The suggestions came pouring in about what other camping gear I should buy to accompany "my" new tent.

This scenario happens to all of us with traditional marketing automation – and it's incredibly off-putting. It might even make us click the "unsubscribe" button or block the business on our social media feeds, which is the kiss of death for any marketing effort. And the quickest way for that to happen is to keep spamming people with irrelevant content.

Adding AI's reasoning to the marketing automation equation results in a different experience. The business will be able to examine my core behavior, not just from one thing I purchased but also from other interests AI can glean, such as social media posts. Instead of taking any single purchase as the gospel of what I like, it will have greater context and likely decide it probably was a one-off buy. Instead of marketing at scale, there will finally be customized marketing to individuals. AI becomes the difference between static or robotic automation and dynamic automation.

The Orchestration of AI and Automation

AI is disrupting automation in the same way it's transforming everything else. The best way to see long-term success during uncertainty is to become good at adapting and handling change. At the same time, it's not as simple as slapping AI into processes and proclaiming "mission accomplished." It will require a new level of orchestration.

In an upcoming chapter, I discuss the essential elements of an AI-driven integration and automation platform in greater detail. But I want to touch on three underlying principles here because they are closely tied to orchestrating a digital architecture through automation.

- Composability
- Democratization
- Visibility and control

Let's briefly take a closer look.

Composability

Composability is about breaking down your digital capabilities into modular components that can be easily assembled, disassembled, and reassembled to meet changing needs. Think of it like LEGO® blocks – each piece is interchangeable and can be used to quickly build whatever you want. In the context of software, this means you can rapidly adapt to market changes by repurposing existing digital assets rather than starting from scratch.

This modular approach allows for faster innovation and greater flexibility. Composable, reusable components are designed to work together seamlessly, enabling your business to respond more efficiently to new opportunities or challenges. You can create and modify applications with less effort, ensuring that your digital infrastructure remains agile and scalable.

Democratization

Barry Gerdsen, one of my colleagues at Boomi, cites a great example of how empowering nontechnical users with a self-service model can completely change an industry: TurboTax®.

Once upon a time, if filing your taxes was too complicated, you had no choice but to hire a CPA. Even when tax preparation software first appeared, it was designed for accountants, not clients. But

TurboTax made tax preparation more manageable for the masses with an interview-style approach for everyone. In other words, it democratized how we do our taxes.

Democratization makes technology more accessible for anyone in the broader organization without waiting for overworked IT teams to do something for them. The more digital builders an organization has, the more capacity exists to do the work – and do it more accurately. An AI-driven integration and automation platform that requires no coding to connect systems and build workflows is a perfect example because it abstracts away the more technical aspects of connectivity.

For instance, the platform enables business analysts to manage their own data projects, which makes perfect sense because they know what they need. IT is no longer a bottleneck, eliminating wasted time and frustration. Technical professionals can be ready to help their "citizen integrator" colleagues when needed, but more of their time can be devoted to weightier projects requiring their expertise. They're more like player-coaches than the help desk. It's a win–win.

Many organizations have already successfully democratized IT. Ivy League school Cornell University[3] is one excellent example. The university comprises more than 15 undergraduate, graduate, and professional colleges and schools, each with its own technical team, supported by departments such as student information, HR, finance, housing, dining, libraries, and athletics. Cornell Information Technologies keeps this small city digitally connected.

"People don't realize how complex a university's architecture can be," said Jeff Christen, Cornell Information Technology's manager for data warehousing and integrations. "Everything is distributed into different departments and colleges. It encompasses hundreds of systems, and all of them have to talk to each other. There's a lot of plumbing."

That means there's a lot of work. Christen's team spreads the load and improves efficiency by using an intelligent integration and automation platform that enables the central IT team to dispense and oversee six sub-accounts maintained by individual departments. While Christen's group is the landlord and holds the keys, other "tenants" are empowered to integrate systems and automate processes as they see fit. As a result of this democratized "citizen development" strategy, projects are completed faster, in the way that the department stakeholders prefer. And whenever problems arise, central IT is ready to help.

"We have a lot of citizen integrators," Christen said. "And it helps that we have a lot of smart people on campus."

It's also smart to share the responsibility for building processes. At the same time, if automation management isn't centralized, it can quickly become a free-for-all where there's little consistency because every department is doing its own thing when it comes to process automation. Here's something else to consider. What if you don't need to build something in the first place because someone else has already created a template you can replicate? This would save time and effort. Sound management keeps everything operating smoothly and reduces the possibility of inadvertent security risks and vulnerabilities. After all, democracy without governance can quickly become anarchy.

This leads us to the final principle.

Visibility and Control

Automation can provide incredible productivity gains and improve our employees' work lives. But it can also run amok if not correctly managed. That problem will only increase in the age of AI. There needs to be a balance between ease of use and federated governance that provides control and security with an end-to-end line of sight into processes.

Consider an example I observed firsthand at iCIMS, the talent cloud company where I was the CEO. Some companies post jobs where they get literally 10,000 applicants for a single position. That number may be on the extreme end, but making it easy to apply for jobs online has meant more resumes that HR teams must parse through for every position. It's no secret that businesses have used automation and traditional machine learning for years to help them deal with that onslaught. Talent acquisition is another fertile area for AI-infused automation to identify top candidates better, and it's something we worked on at iCIMS.

But how do you know, and satisfactorily explain, that AI didn't discriminate in choosing five candidates over the other 9,995 people you didn't select for interviews? What criteria prioritized a select few and deprioritized the rest? What was the model that trained the AI? Was there any unintentional bias involved?

Maybe the model isn't wrong or discriminatory. But how can you prove that if the processes occur in a black box and aren't visible? You need explainability and transparency. But the reality is that the under-the-cover actions are much more opaque with AI. This means extra diligence is required in terms of visibility and control.

Business management legend Peter Drucker often gets the credit for saying, "You can't manage what you can't measure." You also can't manage what you can't see. End-to-end visibility and control with complete security are everything in an increasingly complex IT landscape. The information provided by AI and automation is only valuable if you can show that it's trustworthy and governed by consistent, responsible, and secure policies.

Integration + Automation

Over the last decade-plus, the general idea of digital transformation has been to connect line-of-business applications so they work better together. Automating workflows saves time and money. But AI is bumping up automation's game. For me, practical AI begins with the concept of automating interconnected processes. It's not just improving existing automation but transforming it into something better. It's AI as an ally.

This chapter ends with another pop culture reference. Remember the AI character Jarvis in the Ironman movies?[49] AI is like putting a version of Jarvis on every existing automated process and letting it find even more efficiencies. (Although without the smart-aleck attitude.) Using it to optimize automated processes potentially gives your organization tens of thousands of hours of added productivity. You're freeing up your people to do the tasks worthy of their creativity, not those requiring little thinking. You're providing the gift of time.

But before you take advantage of AI, you must first connect your digital assets to enable the automation of your processes. That's why, again, I say that integration and automation are two sides of the same coin. Both will grow exponentially in importance going forward. The ability to standardize integration and automation to interconnect processes with one platform will be foundational for AI success.

That's the perfect lead-in to my conversation with Betsy Atkins, three-time CEO, who believes that companies that lean into AI now will be best positioned for swifter digital transformation – and that integration and automation are key requirements for everything.

Chapter Takeaway

Three Things to Know

1. Automation is the logical extension of integration. It uses the connections created between systems to create workflows and move data wherever it is needed.

2. Traditional automation has advanced as far as possible because it's brittle and has issues around scalability and adaptability to workflow changes.

3. AI will take automation to the next level by adding reasoning and requiring less human involvement in processes without losing human oversight.

Why It Matters

If you think automation improves productivity throughout your business today, you haven't seen anything yet. AI will play a massive role in supercharging workflow automation, creating even greater efficiencies.

The Bottom Line

Getting more from automation in the age of AI requires identifying repetitive tasks you can streamline for quick wins, prioritizing security around processes, investing in training to ensure your team has the skills to manage and optimize automated systems, and gradually layering in AI to enhance decision-making without overwhelming your infrastructure.

A Conversation with Betsy Atkins

■ ■ ■

Betsy Atkins has more hands-on experience driving business success than most of us can ever hope to achieve. A three-time CEO and serial entrepreneur skilled at launching, building, and scaling companies, Betsy has expertise in both B2B and B2C software. She's participated in 17 IPOs and is an authority on eliminating friction from the consumer experience.

She has served on nearly 40 public boards covering industries including healthcare, financial services, technology, manufacturing, automotive, hospitality, and retail. She currently has several board-room seats, including one at Wynn Resorts. And she literally wrote the book – *Be Board Ready* – about how to become a board member and excel in the role.[50]

Betsy's wealth of experience in reducing costs and driving productivity also informs her thinking on how AI can streamline processes and create organizational efficiencies.

"What boards have figured out is that if they don't lean in and adopt AI and technology, they're going to be left behind," Betsy said at Constellation Research's AI Forum in September 2024.[51]

I was honored that she agreed to this conversation, given her unparalleled perspective on how company boards view digital transformation and AI's game-changing potential for businesses.

Steve Lucas: How do you define digital transformation, and how is it viewed in the boardroom?

Betsy Atkins: Digital transformation is the use of technology to replace legacy processes that haven't been automated. Early on, like in 2010, it was a buzzword to describe an accelerating continuum of change. Then, 10 years ago, streaming arrived, mobile phones passed landlines, Tesla started, and the concept of agile R&D emerged. We take all of those for granted now. But in 2015, boards were still spelling "cyber" with an "S" and not a "C." Companies were buying point solutions to automate parts of their business process flow. But they weren't really thinking of that as "digital transformation." It didn't reach the boardroom until, in my opinion, probably 2020. That's when they finally got it and started to think about it as a category.

SL: That feels both very true and remarkably recent. So then, in your mind, does digital transformation mean something different than it did 10 years ago? Or should it mean something different?

BA: It's radically different, and it should be. Everything changes. If you look at the spend on digital transformation in 2022, it was $1.6 trillion. That's an unbelievable number. Yet in 2026, it's going to be $3.4 trillion.[52] If you're spending that much money, you darn sure want to know if you're getting something for it. COVID was a tectonic shift, as corporations had to figure out how to do business remotely with their customers, engage their employees, and keep productivity levels high. So, for boards, the big question was whether your industry and business models were about to die if you didn't digitally transform.

SL: So, when we say digital transformation today and going forward, it means much more than the automation of a process.

BA: I see that as the big shift. How you process your data in real time is a competitive differentiation, especially with the capabilities of AI and machine-learning algorithms. Consider a customer service use case that makes me buy more products. AI knows I've bought a blue plaid shirt, and maybe I need a sweater to go with it. AI looks me up and says, "Oh, you only bought sweaters in red, orange, and yellow, so maybe you need blue." That kind of predictive suggestion to upsell, cross-sell, and personalize is something that we can do now. Companies that adopt it early will do well. The brands that will win are the ones that fix their user experience, make it easier for me, let me own my data, and respect my privacy. It's the same with B2B, where in the supply chain, AI understands my historical patterns of purchasing and can make suggestions or raise a question. That will make the difference in which companies win and which companies fall behind.

SL: How do you see integration and automation playing a role in digital transformation overall?

BA: I think they're the foundational building blocks. Automating processes has been going on incrementally in manufacturing since Henry Ford. Today, it's faster and more meaningful. But companies that only automate will not win without integration. Yet, I often think people don't really understand what integration is. Having served as a board member at Volvo, I've seen a use case where cars have sensors that tell you if your wheels are vibrating or the road is slippery. But that isn't useful without integrating all these IoT sensors into an active safety system to prevent a collision. It's the same if there's a vibration in my AC or my engine making a weird noise. That's really not very helpful if you don't integrate it and say with a message, "Go to the dealer, or your engine's gonna seize up." Or if you haven't integrated into the dealer's service system to send the parts necessary to repair my car quickly.

A Conversation with Betsy Atkins

So, automation without integration is basically ineffective. Automation that isn't integrated equals a legacy company that will underperform. You simply won't be a viable company if you don't integrate what you have automated.

SL: You must have lots of examples like that from your board work.

BA: At Wynn Resorts, we have automation with a good back-office ERP system. But until we integrate Steve Lucas's information, either when he checks in or creates a loyalty program, we won't have the information needed to give him a personalized experience the next time he stays at one of our properties. We need a special, personalized experience to keep him as a loyal customer versus going to play at our competitors. So, without actually integrating all of our systems, we're going to underperform. We'll be able to serve Steve a cocktail, but if the other guy gives Steve better, personalized incentives, he'll go next door. Value is not created just by having the information. You have to integrate it.

SL: So, from your perspective, value is not created by having the information, whether it's sensors from a tire or someone checking into a hotel. The value is in bringing those multiple fact points together to create the experience.

BA: That's completely correct. And if you listen to boardroom discussions, when it comes to IT, there's crankiness. The board members think, "I spent all this money on software. Why is my business not automatically better?" But they don't know what to ask. It's not just how much you spent on all this enterprise software budget. They never conceptualized how they were going to integrate all these systems to drive insights in real time and use that data. But now it's coming into focus with generative AI because they can see the use cases. Let's say I'm an insurance company, and I have to do a worker's comp claim where my underwriter has a 70-page document and needs to figure out if the person will get a benefit for his shoulder injury. It takes them four to eight hours to go through all those medical forms and documents to make a decision. With generative AI, it literally takes four seconds instead of four hours. AI has read everything, summarized it, and made a recommendation with references to check. The bigger Nirvana lies in integrating the huge investment that companies have made in all these underlying pieces of enterprise software that are best in class: Adobe, Salesforce, ServiceNow – whatever it is. You bought all this stuff, but you don't get all the value until you have added the integration. That's what boards aren't quite focusing on yet. They don't know the questions to ask. But practitioners, like the chief information officers, understand that. And business unit leaders, CMOs, and manufacturing VPs don't know what's missing, but they know they should get more value. And all that is because those systems aren't integrated.

SL: That's a perfect transition into a deeper discussion about AI. Do you believe AI will impact how organizations digitally transform?

BA: AI will absolutely be one of those inflection points. The big change is going to be for the companies that do it first. History has shown that early adopters are the companies that pull ahead while the others are left behind. So, here's an example. I served on the board of Schneider Electric, which most Americans may not have heard of. But today, it's bigger than GE, Honeywell, or Siemens. All those companies were broken up into smaller chunks. But Schneider Electric has left competitors in the dust because they invested in sensor-enabling and machine learning. They acquired software companies. They purposefully, from the top down, made the transition to adopting AI. They have been the winner. The legacy losers are struggling to catch up. AI is moving to this phase where it will transform business processes, like procurement quoting. If you could lower your procurement costs by 15% with AI, that would be huge. Imagine if you're a hardware company and your material costs drop by 15%. That's unbelievable! The companies that develop use cases like those see an early, clear return on investment and will learn faster and perform better. But without integrating data assets, they've lost the power that's the foundation of any of these generative AI use cases.

SL: To further extend that question, what does the future hold for AI? What are the macro changes that you expect to see in the enterprise?

BA: We're going to see a lot more compliance and rigor around data: who uses my data and how my privacy works. It continues to go right back to integration. There will be a giant pull that's going to demand corporations figure out how to use their data assets. You know the data story everybody has heard about: "Oh, I have five versions of how to spell Steve Lucas. What's the golden version?" You need to figure out your data. Maybe you're barely doing it now. But if you don't do it, you're going to die. With generative AI use cases, there's a more important role that integration is going to perform, which people don't understand yet. It's a complex, really hard problem of integrating all of your assets and making them usable, which will keep you competitive as a company.

SL: We're at the point where everyone is trying to figure out how to find and derive real value from AI. And I firmly believe that the road will be littered with the next generation of Blockbuster Videos that just did not move quickly enough.

BA: We used to say that the rate of change was geometric. Now, it's exponential, and we're headed toward quantum.

Summary

If you want to know how the board of directors at major businesses view digital transformation and AI, this is it right here. Betsy is thinking about the practicality of AI. And boards are nothing if not practical. They need to see value in any initiative. This is why I find it so interesting that Betsy gravitates toward real business outcomes when she talks about AI. We can all talk about the amazing possibilities of AI. However, there must always be proven results and value to support the massive technology investments.

Chapter 5

API Management: Optimizing Connectivity for AI

What we discuss in this chapter:

- APIs are the connective tissue of the digital world and the quiet engine that has helped power the global economy for the last 15-plus years.

- APIs will become even more pervasive within your business as the link between AI's large language models and autonomous processes. This requires you to reimagine how you think about API management.

- The Credit Union of Colorado is a great example of a financial institution that protects its members by making data accessible through intelligent connectivity, including APIs.

"It's about caring for people as individuals."

Large-scale wildfires have become a common occurrence in the western United States. On the night of December 30, 2021, a grass fire exploded, driven by wind gusts as strong as 115 miles per hour, and rapidly spread across Boulder County, Colorado.

Fortunately, a heavy snowfall extinguished the flames from the Marshall fire before it could become more destructive. Still, 40,000 people fled their homes, and more than 1,000 structures burned down, causing $2 billion in damage.

"It was very personal to me because my close neighbors were evacuated," said Mitch Rosenbaum, the Senior Vice President of Marketing and Digital Services for the Credit Union of Colorado.

In those early hours, when neighborhoods were still in jeopardy, the credit union was already contacting members. The technical team generated a report using membership data to map out who might be in harm's way and quickly reach out to them. The message was simple: We're here for you.

"In many cases, people said we were the first phone call they got, and they appreciated that we were offering support," Rosenbaum said. "It turned out that those wildfires didn't directly impact a significant group of our members. But it shows our core value of trying to help people and being ready if they have financial hardships, like the flexibility to skip a payment or offer grants for short-term needs like groceries or a place to live."

The Credit Union of Colorado[53] could respond like that because Boomi's AI-driven integration and automation platform is at the heart of the company's technical architecture.

"We were able to leverage data we've collected in our data warehouse using APIs and move it to a system that allows us to connect with our members," added Jacob Hoffman, Service Delivery Manager, Enterprise Applications. "People don't need the added stressors like mortgage payments when they're already in devastating situations for a family. Our data and analytics team does an amazing job of using technology to paint a picture of our members and understanding how we can help support them."

Banks that are "too big to fail" are often in the news for all the wrong reasons. However, credit unions are the feel-good story in the highly competitive financial market. These are regional, not-for-profit financial institutions owned and controlled by their members. They've grown steadily in recent years, with over 135 million members in 2022.[54]

Part of their appeal is that consumers are attracted to lower fees and strong interest rates. It's also because credit unions have a personal touch. The staff knows members' names and can deliver more personalized services. There are no investors to please with higher profits, only members to make happy. The sole focus is helping people create better financial security and their communities thrive.

The Credit Union of Colorado exemplifies that people-first niche in the financial industry. A mid-sized institution founded in 1934 and based in Denver, the organization has expanded to more than 17,000 members with over $2.5 billion in assets. However, while credit unions are growing in popularity, there is also a less rosy story. Most consumers use more than one financial institution today, and surveys show they still consider large banks the primary choice. One reason credit unions are seen as the "backup" is a perception that they can't match the technology capabilities of big banks.

The Credit Union of Colorado has worked hard to change that sentiment by embarking on an ambitious digital transformation effort to meet – and exceed – consumers' expectations with easy-button-style services. That meant addressing a connectivity issue around the core banking system used by most credit unions. This system was designed in the late 1980s and early 1990s when members always came to a physical location and stepped up to the window.

It didn't keep pace with digital banking and proved difficult to integrate with new financial solutions designed for interoperability through APIs. The business was limited in the type of best-of-breed technology it could deploy based on what the core system enabled through preferred vendors. The Credit Union of Colorado was constrained by less nimble solutions that fit the arbitrary criteria of the core banking vendor, not cloud solutions that best suit the members' needs.

"The bottom line is that expectations are driven by the mobile device," Rosenbaum said. "People want the ability to get a loan immediately and to make transactions at a moment's notice. It's our job to provide ease of use because that's what consumers expect from our services."

Adopting the Boomi Enterprise Platform in 2020 gave the credit union flexibility to choose member-centric services that were previously impossible by providing a secure layer of connectivity with the core banking system and bridging the gap between legacy and modern applications. That meant integrations for systems that include digital banking, member service, marketing automation, and more. It enabled:

- More self-service interactions, like from mobile devices. That includes services such as e-statements, Zelle payments, and online loan applications – with decisions made in minutes.

- A loan-decision platform tailored for credit unions, which provides a deeper analysis for approving loans based on behavioral models.

- An analysis solution that proactively offers more personalized services to each member by tapping into the information in the data warehouse.

- Better fraud detection capabilities to quickly notify members of unusual account activity.

The behind-the-scenes technology ensures that the Credit Union of Colorado is always there for members. This was the case during the pandemic, when, thanks to the new analytic tools, the credit union could determine which members were eligible to skip loan payments if they had difficulty making ends meet.

"We were able to deliver a clear message to members that we were ready to help," Rosenbaum said. "Then, with one click, they could skip a payment. For us, that's about personal outreach. It's about caring for people as individuals."

Key Points

- **Goal:** Create seamless connectivity between legacy and modern systems, giving members the low-friction digital experiences they expect and enabling the organization to make more informed decisions based on the best data.

- **Human Impact:** About 140 integrations across legacy, cloud, and fintech partner systems have enabled the credit union to deliver on its promise to always be there for members. A new digitally provided member experience contributed to a 5% leap in NPS scores.[55] Also, they created integrations nearly five times faster. This was partly due to eliminating costly, time-consuming professional services from application vendors and the tangle of point-to-point connections that were difficult to maintain and customize by a five-person technical team.

- **Lessons Learned:** "One of the big lessons for me is making sure we have technologies in place that allow us to have a broader bucket of vendors we can integrate with. That means being very diligent in those conversations and being educated. We learned to really understand what we're getting ourselves into, so we're not pigeonholing ourselves with a solution that may not be meeting the needs of our organization." – *Jacob Hoffman, Service Delivery Manager, Enterprise Applications, Credit Union of Colorado*

"Previously, we were built for large-scale project implementations. We'd take three to five years and roll them out only when they were as close to perfect as we could get them. We've created a much more modern approach to development. We'll take a limited scope, implement, and iterate. We move a lot faster." – *Mitch Rosenbaum, Senior Vice President of Marketing and Digital Services for the Credit Union of Colorado*

The Hidden Influence of APIs

You may be wondering, "Why are we even having a conversation about APIs?" Well, APIs are how all systems speak to each other in our modern world. If you want to share information securely and intelligently, APIs are the way to go.

APIs are precisely, as the name suggests, interfaces between software applications. By acting as digital gateways, they abstract away technical complexity and promote flexible, plug and play development and integration. They enable different software systems to communicate with each other by acting as go-betweens. APIs provide rules and protocols that define how software systems share information without needing to know each other's inner workings. Applications essentially "expose" their functionality through API gateways to provide structured data movement.

You already know this if you're in IT. If you're not, know that APIs are essential and can make a massive difference for your business. I also promise you it's a much more captivating topic than you might think. This is because your ability to manage APIs will go a long way in determining just how successful you are in making your business AI-ready. This is make-or-break stuff.

If you're already well-versed in this technology, just skim through the next section about the ABCs of APIs.

Here are three reasons why you should care about APIs.

1. The world's modern technology systems talk through the language of APIs.

2. You have no idea how many APIs are in your business, what they do, who uses them, or whether they pose security risks.

3. Building new digital applications typically involves incorporating data from existing systems via APIs.

It's an API world, and we're just living in it. You might not realize it, but everything digital runs on APIs. They're ubiquitous in our modern lives, quietly working their connectivity magic behind the scenes. I'm sure you've seen the classic movie *The Matrix*. Near the end of the film, the protagonist, Neo, finally sees the world around him as it really is – written in code. You should look at the world the same way. Pretty much everything we use or touch nowadays is somewhat driven by code and APIs.

Every time you interact with something on the Internet, APIs are there. They're how you have seamless shopping experiences online, access your favorite apps, schedule rideshares, watch shows on streaming services, and so much more. One report released in 2024 found that 71% of all Internet traffic consists of API calls.[56] There's a reason why the phrase "the API Economy" exists.

Put simply, APIs are the means of exchange in a world where data is currency. They're strictly transactional.

For instance, if I want to know today's weather in my hometown of Denver, I open the weather app on my iPhone. An "API call" acts like a messenger and requests the Apple Weather Service's API. It automatically retrieves that snippet of local weather information (temperature, humidity, forecast, etc.) and sends it back to my phone app without me knowing that the connection has even

API Management: Optimizing Connectivity for AI

occurred. Because the API serves as an information bridge between the weather service and my iPhone, I'll know if I need an umbrella today. Although we like to say in Colorado that if you don't like the weather, just wait 15 minutes because it will change.

Or consider when I'm hungry and don't want to hit the drive-thru for a cup of that chili from my favorite fast-food restaurant. I also frequent a particular sandwich shop near my home. And by "frequent," I mean ordering through DoorDash.

The simple task of ordering a sandwich requires an extraordinarily complex series of digital actions that involve orchestrating a small army of APIs. When I place the order, DoorDash must confirm the transaction with a third party – the restaurant. Can they make the sandwich? It must also identify the closest available DoorDash driver via GPS location data. It needs to calculate the cost, tax, and driver fee. It needs to tell me when I can expect delivery. All of this is happening in near real time. Oh, and it also needs to provide the ability for the driver to communicate with me via text messages.

Getting my tasty sandwich while it's still fresh requires navigating an insane number of digital interactions made possible by APIs around order placement, order management, payment, communication, and delivery.

Those are just two commonplace examples. APIs provide access to an infinite range of services that impact each of us daily. Our mobile devices are chock full of APIs. Without them, we'd be back in the days when mobile phones were only used to make and receive calls.

Matt McLarty, whom I introduced in Chapter 3, has been at the forefront of the API movement since their influence emerged in the first decade of the 2000s. Few people have followed the growth of APIs more closely. He co-hosts *The API Experience* podcast[57] and has talked extensively about how API use exploded from niche technology to indispensability with the popularity of mobile device apps and social networks. This placed newfound importance on API management tools for developers to write, test, create documentation, and use. From there, APIs expanded into the realm of internal integrations, leading to layered architectures, which needed a different kind of API lifecycle policy enforcement. Then came the next step of the evolution, which was cloud-native API management and working with event-driven microservices and containers.

Suddenly, the API economy was a thing. But now, it's about to get even bigger. The breadth of APIs is expanding with the rise of AI.

In their recent book, *Unbundling the Enterprise*, McLarty and coauthor Steven Fishman say, "The rise of social networks was API-enabled. A critical factor in Facebook's early dominance was its 'Like' button, which was built on top of the Facebook Graph API. Mobile apps were built on data and functions coming from cloud services via APIs. Even today's AI boom is largely dependent on APIs. Generative AI is being incorporated into customer experiences through APIs, and corporations are embedding their own services into third-party models via API."[58]

So, we live in an API-driven world. (I realize, in retrospect, I could have saved some time by just moving on after I said that at the beginning. But now we're all on the same page.) You might be thinking, "That's great, Steve – good to know! But I presume you will now tell us there's a problem, right?"

Yes, indeed. There's a massive problem. How do you manage all these darn things?

The API Sprawl Problem

It's widely accepted that large enterprises have hundreds, if not thousands, of APIs. I wish I could cite a trusted source to back up this assertion. But here's the reality. It's impossible to say how many exist from business to business because nobody can tell exactly what they have.

You just don't know.

It's like somebody asking me how many neurons are in my brain. I don't know. A lot, I guess? Ask me the follow-up question about what percentage of those neurons I use. Again, I don't know. Maybe 10%? All I can tell you for certain from what I've observed in life is that some people seem to use far fewer neurons than others.

Joking aside, you can draw an analogy between what I'm facetiously saying about neurons and the reality of APIs within organizations. There are APIs in your organization, whether your IT team created them, or they're embedded in third-party applications that are entirely unmanaged. This is why you have no idea how many you have, who uses them, or whether they are secure.

Your first step toward managing your APIs probably should be discussing API *discovery*. API discovery tools can tell you what APIs you have – even the ones you didn't know you had. That's the 90% of the brain you aren't using.

Now, maybe your response is: "But wait, Steve. We have an API management tool! We've got this covered!" Well, you don't. Not fully, anyway.

You may have one API management platform or potentially two. Maybe five. Possibly even more than that. Now, we're starting to get to the heart of the API problem:

1. You don't know how many APIs you have and where they are across all your systems, databases, and devices.

2. You're inefficiently managing the APIs that you do know about.

What you lack, again, is a single, holistic platform that manages and secures all your APIs in one place.

So, the term "API management" is a misnomer. The truth is that most enterprises only think they're managing APIs. At best, management happens only within pockets inside organizations. It's anyone's guess how many are actively being managed and how many are falling through the cracks. If you're in IT, I suspect you probably know this nagging feeling firsthand.

As I asserted, APIs are everywhere, partly because architectures have become so much more complicated with migrations to multi-cloud environments, continued reliance on legacy on-premises systems, and the explosion of third-party applications. Also, APIs aren't created equally. They're not all secure or well-managed. They're not all enabled for the best usage or optimized for performance. Perhaps worst of all, an organization doesn't have a way to see all the APIs, which creates security risks.

The API dilemma is the same theme we keep returning to throughout this book about applications and data: fragmentation. Once upon a time, in the early days of API management, there was centralized control of a few API products by a select group of people with technical expertise who oversaw building, publishing, and managing them. But with the growth of the API economy and digital transformation, that pesky genie has broken out of the bottle, and it's not going back. That's why little rhyme, reason, or consistency exists for managing APIs within the typical business.

Welcome to API sprawl! This free-for-all presents a multitude of problems that limit the value your business is supposed to see from them, which include:

- **Lack of Governance:** Different API technologies are scattered across the enterprise, operating independently. One team might use cloud-native gateways with new APIs built on AWS or Microsoft Azure. However, other lines of business might use different API management tools designed for on-premises needs. This kind of heterogeneity is a fact of life today. On the one hand, it helps groups work more independently and faster.

141

API Management: Optimizing Connectivity for AI

But there are costs. A 2023 Forrester survey found that 57% of companies reported challenges related to having API gateways managed by more than one vendor.[59] Remember, democratization without governance can lead to anarchy.

- **Shadow APIs:** Can the CIO say their team has an accurate, complete view of all the active APIs on their network? It's highly unlikely. There are many reasons why unmanaged "zombie APIs" wander the digital landscape. People build and publish APIs and then leave the company. Teams create APIs for a project and forget to turn them off when it ends. APIs can easily get lost in the shuffle until a problem surfaces.

- **Technical Debt:** Teams building APIs with multiple tools without knowing what others already created inevitably leads to redundancies and higher costs. There's just more stuff you don't need in your digital architecture. This also increases complexity in the digital environment because there are more things to maintain and rationalize. Having a bunch of API managers to watch over all the different fiefdoms is an expensive luxury that most IT departments don't have.

- **Security Risks:** Unmanaged APIs are magnets for bad actors. They're the keys to the vaults regarding sensitive data. One report published in 2023 found that 29% of web attacks targeted APIs because cybercriminals know they're sometimes published without adequate security protocols.[60] Another security study in 2023 determined that 74% of organizations reported at least three API-related data breaches over the previous two years.[61] Yet, too often, businesses don't even want to know if there are vulnerabilities because they fear what they might find if they look. It's like having your basement flood but saying, "Well, as long as I don't go down there and check, I'm sure there isn't a problem." But there's probably water damage, no matter how hard you pretend it doesn't exist. Unsecured APIs can also cause serious havoc.

- **Lack of Use:** APIs have zero business value if they're unused. There's no return on your API investment. You've put effort into their design, creation, deployment, and operation. Now you're letting many of them gather dust? What's the point? Even more frustrating is when another team comes along and spends the time and money to build the exact same thing you already have!

This is why the goal of consistent, secure, and well-governed APIs that drive innovation systematically is a pipe dream within businesses. In theory, APIs should add value. Instead, they're more likely to add complexity and risk. API sprawl has become the digital Wild West.

Bringing order to this chaos requires a new kind of sheriff.

Thinking About API Management Differently

The paradigm of traditional API management is over. It had a nice run, but the toolkit is ill-suited to address the next level challenges of API sprawl – from technological and organizational perspectives. It's not working for your business now, and it doesn't have the right stuff for what's coming next. If you think APIs are everywhere now, just wait until AI hits its stride. APIs will be the fundamental connectivity in the AI ecosystem for reasons I'll explain. And API sprawl will increase exponentially.

The game has to change as the API economy grows to support the AI economy. You require a more practical way of thinking about API management.

You need *federated API governance* (Figure 5.1).

API Management: Optimizing Connectivity for AI

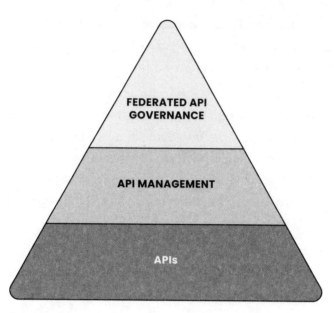

Figure 5.1 Federated API governance provides control over API management and individual APIs.

OK, I admit that name doesn't sound very cool. So, let's think of it like legendary fantasy author J. R. R. Tolkien would. Federated API governance is the proverbial "one ring to rule them all." Still, "federated" is the crucial word here. It means unifying independent entities under a central, overarching framework while maintaining individual autonomy. It's the ability to control many different API management technologies from one point of view and through a single lens.

Of course, you might think the obvious solution to an API sprawl problem is for your brightest minds to get together in a room or on a Zoom call, have a long discussion, and settle on one API management platform for the entire enterprise. Good luck with that! It will never happen. You'll never just pick one and decommission the rest. It isn't practical or realistic in our heterogeneous technology landscapes. Teams want what they want. But what if those different API gateways had a single gatekeeper keeping them all in line, watching for problems, and even looking for rogue or forgotten APIs that might be ripe targets for hackers?

Hence, the one ring that rules all those other rings.

A federated API governance control plane is an approach that provides the end-to-end consistency, compliance, and visibility across a complex ecosystem. Here's how.

Centralized Control and Decentralized Autonomy

Federated management brings balance to "Middle Earth" API governance. It provides centralized standards for the entire organization while allowing individual teams some independence with the authority to create, deploy, and maintain APIs according to their own requirements and timelines. This holistic approach ensures the enterprise is marching to the beat of the same API drum in terms of policies, security, etc. Yet teams can keep using the technology that suits their individual needs. It's the best of both worlds.

With a single view, APIs are standardized and visible in one place, and other teams can easily reuse those already built. This availability and reusability are the hallmarks of composability. When they're at everyone's fingertips, it increases their use of your API portfolio. This translates to quicker time to value and the ability for the business to adjust to changing circumstances faster. It also encourages democratization because nontechnical team members know there's a safety net to protect them as they build and use APIs. Finally, that visibility also makes it easier to troubleshoot problems and measure meaningful analytics in an organized fashion.

Most importantly, federated management allows you to herd all your API cats (or maybe that should be hobbits.)

API Security

For as long as the API economy has existed, security breaches have been a problem. Part of the issue is the ethos of APIs. You make and publish APIs to encourage widespread use. It's a very open concept. But with great use comes the potential for greater risk. Too often, security hasn't been given enough focus in the API lifecycle. However, the value of a federated governance system is that you have greater transparency in your API portfolio. It's the antidote for risk. More visibility equals more security. It also allows you to address problems faster when vulnerabilities do arise.

Just as important, a federated governance system includes standardized requirements to ensure that every API you release meets your level of governance needs. For companies in regulated industries such as healthcare or finance, it's mandatory to follow strict data security and privacy regulations. But who am I kidding? It's a must for every organization in today's world.

The last thing any company wants to do is issue a press release about a customer data breach that gets sourced back to an unsecured API. That would ruin anyone's day.

API Discovery

Have you ever watched a documentary about the human brain where it shows how neurons and synapses will fire based on their reaction to different stimuli? What if you could map the "brain" of your organization to locate different APIs and their location by how they fire?

In other words, what if you could finally identify all the APIs in your organization? Don't you want to know what data or access you're opening up to your business partners? Or what APIs sit within your firewall, potentially leaking data and creating that next high-profile breach headline?

Understanding the universe of APIs is incredibly important to knowing what you use, which ones need limited access, and which ones probably need decommissioning because they're not worth your IT team's valuable management time.

Think of a federated API control plane as an airport control tower with insights into all the APIs flying around your business. It can track your APIs like air traffic controllers keep tabs on passenger jets to keep everyone safe. Or think about a Google search: every time you type in a search term, Google crawls the web and provides you with the results that best match your query. A federated control plane can "crawl" your organization to find all the APIs in your business and identify the risks they pose.

This kind of API management curtails complexity and fragmentation so you can finally have a true sense of what's happening within the organization to make decisions that drive the business forward. Getting the most from APIs requires first bringing them together in a way that gives you all you need to incorporate functionality into your applications. Now, that doesn't sound hard – but don't forget the fact that your APIs are all in different systems. True federated API governance allows you to create these more comprehensive API packages from disparate API management solutions *and* gives you easy, scalable, and centralized management for all of them.

This matters because if you can't wrangle your APIs effectively now, you won't be able to manage the massive upheavals we're already experiencing around AI. But when done correctly, you'll have a competitive differentiator between you and your market rivals.

There's No AI Without APIs

As AI dominates the tech world's focus, the role of APIs will only increase. Why? Think of it this way:

1. AI needs data.

2. APIs supply data.

As the primary connectivity channel for large language model providers, APIs are fundamental to injecting AI into your business processes. When LLM-infused applications provide agents with what they need to act, the process is executed via API calls. Agents, those industrious digital worker bees of the AI economy, don't use human language to talk to each other. They communicate through APIs. This is their language.

This is why talking about API management is far from dull and why you should be incredibly interested in harnessing its full power. The AI economy is very much an API economy. APIs are crucial because they connect AI models to all business systems and serve as conduits for the data fueling those engines. Every organization will need APIs to tap into the vast possibilities of AI. That's why prioritizing the need to manage APIs in the age of AI is crucial. The more API-ready you are, the better prepared you'll be to implement AI.

The way we've managed APIs until now has been very utilitarian. It's been a case of, "I need a thing, and an API will do it for me." Most APIs are built not for a specific business outcome but for a technology-specific set of reasons: reliability, scalability, authentication, authorization, etc. We've never managed them on an outcome basis. Yet the number-one outcome for any business is maintaining customer attention. You need a vision for creating and managing APIs focused on business outcomes rather than technology requirements.

Every business connects applications and databases because we want to achieve goals by automating processes and getting data to those needing it. At the beginning of this chapter, I shared how the Credit Union of Colorado uses data access with the help of APIs to look out for the best interests of its members. APIs are fundamental to creating interconnected processes to make outcomes like that possible. They will be at the forefront of doing the same thing by connecting another business object that's becoming fundamental to our businesses: AI agents.

In the next chapter, we examine the impact agents will have on your business in more detail. But I'll leave you with one Easter egg here.

Sooner than you think, an API management agent will know every API in your organization. It will know your core objectives and priorities, security, scale, reliability, compliance, and whatever else is needed to manage them. It will be able to explain all of them to you, where they're from, what they do, and how they work. And it will be completely autonomous. You'll have one intelligence that's managing the hundreds or thousands of APIs in your ecosystem.

It's just a matter of time.

But for now, my top-line message is that you need to manage your APIs before making your AI dreams come true. You might be eager to get your hands on AI turbo engines and implement them in every part of your business. But it won't matter how many great agents you have if you lack the data to fuel them. Connecting the right data to the right place at the right time requires APIs. That's the sense of urgency you should feel because understanding your APIs will help you better understand AI.

Once you accomplish that, you'll have greater peace of mind knowing that your APIs are secure as they feed potentially sensitive data to your proprietary AI models.

Then, you'll be ready to go big with AI.

Chapter Takeaway

Three Things to Know

1. Traditional API management is outdated and not designed for the AI-led world that businesses are now beginning to navigate.

2. AI agents will use APIs to communicate with one another as their foothold and importance grows within organizations like yours.

3. A new API management strategy will require federated governance, which will manage all APIs in one place, provide greater scalability and security, and enable people without technical expertise to create value with them.

Why It Matters

APIs will connect and infuse AI's large language models with your own high-quality, proprietary data, creating autonomous business processes that will become key competitive differentiators.

The Bottom Line

API management is no longer a niche technical tool that only matters to IT. Getting the most from APIs will directly impact your business' AI implementation success and competitiveness in a changing marketplace.

Chapter 6

Agent Management: The AI Future Is Here

What we discuss in this chapter:

- AI agents are software entities that use AI to perform tasks or services autonomously or semi-autonomously on behalf of humans based on programming, learned behavior, and data inputs.

- Agents are already beginning to handle functions within businesses and will soon manage a multitude of tasks to make organizations more productive, which will free up people for more creative work.

- How the Tropicana juice company used connectivity to meet tight deadlines for creating a standalone digital architecture to support a newly independent company.

"Our digital juice runs through Boomi."

When you think of orange juice, iconic consumer brand Tropicana immediately comes to mind.

Tropicana has been a familiar sight on grocery shelves and an essential breakfast staple for nearly eight decades. Yet Tropicana Brands Group (TBG)[62] has only existed since 2022. The brand, which is also the maker of Naked Smoothies, Izze, and Kevita, became a standalone company when PepsiCo sold a majority portion of the business to the private equity firm PAI Partners.

The formation of TBG was an opportunity to build a new organization that would unleash growth and possibilities with a bold ambition: Be the undisputed global leader in the chilled and fresh beverage category.

An agile, modern technology ecosystem was essential to achieve this goal.

"Our leadership team used a fun analogy in describing our transformation," recalled Jeff Lischett, TBG's Global CIO. "We described it as 'moving out of mom and dad's house.' It pulled the team together and unified a clear intention in building our own capabilities – built by us, for us."

The transformation extended beyond technology and included extensive work across talent, customer management, corporate functions, and marketing/brands. But specific to technology, Lischett's team faced a Herculean task. It only had approximately 18 months to build a dedicated TBG technology ecosystem, including the required talent, systems, processes, services, infrastructure, and equipment separate from PepsiCo's operations.

"Our organization possesses the spirit of a start-up and lives entrepreneurial values," Lischett said. "We are data-driven and leverage technology to maximize our results."

Building that digital foundation was a vital part of the business strategy. In fact, TBG chose a meaningful name for the daunting transition: Project Harvest.

"It symbolized the growth of a new company," Lischett added. "Harvest was about new beginnings. It was an incredible privilege to create a technology core for our incredible people and brands."

From an outcome perspective, the focus was always on people. They needed to ensure employees were prepared for the transition with an effective change management strategy and training, while providing everything required to keep making the best products. Additionally, collaborating with retail partners was critical for TBG to ensure the transition was planned and executed flawlessly.

"There are many different playbooks on how to handle a business carve-out," Lischett said.

TBG chose perhaps the most exciting one. The company took a greenfield approach, building an entirely new digital architecture based on two principles: simplicity and speed. To do this, TBG relied on key strategic technology partnerships, including Boomi. The Boomi Enterprise Platform serves as the integration layer connecting the enterprise. Boomi's EDI capabilities enabled TBG to link with trading partners across its retail and supplier network. As a middleware platform, it knits together order fulfillment execution, supporting the flow of data in and out of the organization's ERP and various core systems that underpin business operations. This means orders are processed, deliveries are executed, and the business partner network is connected – every day, all day, in North America and Europe.

Lischett noted, "Our digital juice runs through Boomi."

TBG met its audacious timelines for launching its global systems, while also building a closer working relationship between IT and the lines of business.

"Building a global platform creates the needed flexibility, and agility to build, optimize, and realize our business strategy," Lischett added. "Despite the focus on technology, the incredible people, key partner contributions, and our relentless execution focus from across the organization were the reason for our success."

Post-divestiture, TBG is preparing for ways to implement AI throughout the business. The starting point is teaching effective, responsible use and applying governance factoring data privacy and ethics. Lischett describes TBG's approach to AI as "human-centered."

"We're all navigating the complexity in understanding and harnessing AI," he said. "AI will be ever-present, and the best versions of it will be hardly noticeable. It will be built natively into hardware operating systems such as our smartphones, extend into business platforms, and be customized to find differentiation. The key at this moment in time is to prepare our organization on how to use it responsibly and effectively and apply it to create value. That includes my personal belief in creating the greatest gift of all: time."

Key Points

- **Goal:** Leverage clean, modern technology platforms to eliminate expensive complexity and accelerate its transformation journey in building the digital tools required for TBG.

- **Human Impact:** TBG met the challenge of a compact go-live schedule in developing a full-scale IT operation. The company prioritized its employees and customers to prepare for the significant changes and mitigated the risks to ensure TBG's juice products continued being produced and in the hands of consumers. Among the many accomplishments of the transition, TBG installed front-to-back IT operations, including security operations, technical services (hosting and network), service desk, managed service partners, physical equipment deployments, cloud development, and a Global ERP implementation. Finally, it developed an industry-leading technical staff.

- **Lessons Learned:** "Where to start. First, an organization must pull together to achieve an outcome of this scale. There were no special interests. This was binary – success or failure. And we couldn't fail. Second, the principles were clear. As an example, speed was non-negotiable, and we created a platform to enable decisions. Lastly, change management doesn't end with the change itself. In some regards, that's when the change management starts. Prepare for the first six months similarly to the previous six months before a go-live. That's because the role and value of change management never really ends." – *Jeff Lischett, Global Chief Information Officer, Tropicana Brands Group*

Strategic Integration and Automation

Throughout this book, I've avoided talking too much about my company. But in this case, I can't help myself. When Jeff said, "The juice runs through Boomi" on stage at an event in 2024 (unscripted, I might add), I vowed to have T-shirts printed with the catchphrase. We've repeated it probably 10,000 times so far. It never gets old.

There are several reasons why I have so much respect for the Tropicana Brand Group team. First, I know from experience the hardship of a divestiture. I've worked at companies of all sizes — those that evolved from start-ups, medium-sized businesses, and massive enterprises. But the hardest thing I've ever done, by far, is carve out a business from a global company. You're implementing systems, procedures, and processes from scratch, on the fly, and in a hurry. You also have to break large company habits that won't work for a smaller, more agile business.

What's so impressive about TBG is that even while the clock was ticking, the company's IT team was strategic about creating a connected infrastructure to make the business more efficient both during the transition and over the long run.

Often, when people are trying to solve business problems, they tend to fixate on applications. They think, "I need an app for invoicing." Or accounting or anything else. I need, I need, I need. The problem is that when you say "I need" 300-plus times and get an application, you end up with this big hot mess in your architecture. The most consequential question for any business should be: "How do I create a connected architecture where all my systems can talk to each other?" TBG built its infrastructure to do exactly that.

Jeff also said something profound that I want to highlight. He mentioned how the integration platform brought together IT and the lines of businesses in a new way, enabling them to collaborate more effectively. We all know what it's like when the partnership between technical and business teams devolves into an us-versus-them situation. It can get ugly.

Because each has a different focus, it can sometimes seem like IT is from Mars and the business is from Venus. However, integration can act like relationship counseling and end the finger-pointing by serving as a bridge between them, helping them achieve the company's collective goals faster and more efficiently.

Finally, I admire Jeff's thoughtful approach to AI and his focus on how it will help people – not necessarily the technology itself. That's incredibly important because the business world is drastically changing.

Agents Are Among Us

It's worth repeating that AI is hardly new. Credible research toward concepts like ChatGPT began at least in the early 1980s. But what has made this remarkable moment in time possible is the convergence of those decades of research and the emergence of new technologies such as powerful GPU-based computers, ubiquitous cloud computing, and access to near-infinite data on the Internet for use as training sets.

A steady, unrelenting march of powerful algorithms and machine learning got us to this point. For instance, take Google's introduction of an image search and recognition capability in 2009. It was the first time we could paste a photo of something into the search bar, like an apple, and Google would tell us: That's an apple. That trick required humans to write an algorithm that translated images into zeros and ones. Then, machine learning took over as we helped teach the algorithm by providing feedback. Maybe it would look at the apple and tell us, "That's a giraffe." When we corrected it, "No, this is an apple," the algorithm gradually learned and improved because it was incentivized to provide correct answers. The algorithm got "points," so to speak, for being right.

That was long before generative AI, but you could see the path where we were heading. Then, in 2017, a clear signpost came that we were nearing a giant leap forward. That was when the famous scientific paper written by eight Google researchers titled "Attention Is All You Need" was published. It's widely viewed as the founding document of the generative AI era because it put forth the idea of predictive transformers.[63] That pattern recognition technology was the basis of OpenAI's thunderclap announcement in late 2022 when it introduced the world to ChatGPT and launched the tidal wave of conversational chatbots (Figure 6.1). (I will again admit that I was caught completely off-guard by ChatGPT's debut.)

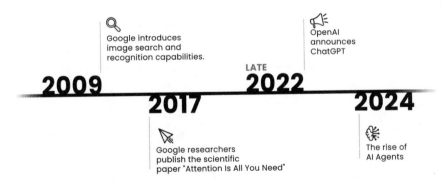

Figure 6.1 A steady, unrelenting march of powerful algorithms and machine learning.

Agent Management: The AI Future Is Here

Through the power of large language models (LLMs), which have been trained on a massive amount of data to understand and generate human-like text, these chatbots can (mostly) answer questions and perform functions in a conversational style. At the highest level, the idea behind the chatbots is simple: input, model, output. You ask a question (input), an algorithm (LLM) considers it, and then, near-instantaneously, gives you an answer (output). These sophisticated algorithms are trained on data to recognize patterns and perform specific tasks such as summarizing information, generating text, writing code, etc. Gradually, they're providing more accurate answers based on a virtuous feedback loop with humans helping to train them.

This is the core of intelligent systems. But LLMs don't just do things on their own. They still require humans.

But with the evolution of AI happening at breathtaking speed, we now have autonomous and semi-autonomous agents designed to perform specific tasks. They use the intelligence from the models and, based on the scope of their programming, can largely take independent action to complete objectives.

1. They're given instructions to do something.

2. They're not told how to do their jobs.

3. They figure out how to achieve the tasks.

In the first chapter, I told you that AI agents are pieces of software that can mimic human activity. They are AI-infused software entities designed to perform jobs, make decisions, and interact with environments or users based on data, predefined rules, and learned patterns. They can tap into systems and data to complete their work, like surfacing requested information. Agents can range from simple chatbots to advanced AI assistants that can run complex workflows.

I know, I know. You might think we've gone from the practical and pragmatic to the theoretical by jumping to agents. But as I've been saying – they're already here, and to stay competitive, you need to know how to harness their power.

"Agency," or the ability to make decisions, requires a cognitive ability that has always been the domain of human intelligence. At least, that's what we used to think. Not anymore. Yes, agents use the guidance of humans, who interact with them through typing or speaking commands. However, agents are software with "brains" that can act iteratively. They choose actions on their own and make decisions by tapping into data sources from numerous applications – helping guide the direction of your business. They don't follow deterministic, if–then–else pathways. They are free to execute tasks. And agents aren't just execution engines. They're automating the steps to accomplish those tasks faster and more efficiently.

Some characteristics of agents include:

- Making decisions using AI-based reasoning
- Acting independently of human intervention
- Having defined scopes of activity
- Working alone or in conjunction with other AI agents
- Having a specific personality

By the way, the difference between autonomous agents and semi-autonomous agents depends on the level of human involvement in their use. But they all mimic human activity. And there's one other thing you should know. Agents will soon be everywhere in your business. A 2024 global survey of 1,100 executives conducted by the Capgemini Research Institute found that while only 10% of organizations were using agents, 82% said they intended to integrate them into their processes in one to three years.[64] Meanwhile, companies such as Salesforce, Oracle, Google, and ServiceNow are rolling out "agentic" features. Also, Gartner predicts that one-third of all interactions with generative AI services to complete tasks will involve autonomous agents by 2028.[65]

We've already seen how rapidly businesses have adopted conversational chatbot models to automate content creation, improve decision-making processes, and personalize customer interactions. But that's just the beginning.

We're now seeing next-generation agents emerge as orchestrators of complex actions. In two years, if not sooner, agents will be a business element that's as much a part of our infrastructure as APIs, databases, and applications. You'll be able to conduct reasonably advanced conversations with agents that direct them to go out and accomplish work with minimal human oversight. They will operate on your behalf, and you won't think twice about it. We'll collaborate with these agents similarly to how we work with our human colleagues on projects. Human attention is limited and valuable. Agent assistants will let us focus on essentials that require our creativity. I'll even take it another step further. In less than three years, the number of AI agents within your business will outnumber your employees.[66]

Microsoft co-founder Bill Gates has written extensively about the power of agents.[67] He envisions personal agents that can help us accomplish a wide range of tasks, such as assisting us in booking travel that fits our budgets and is personalized with what we like to do because they know our preferences. Unlike the infamous "Clippy," the annoying and much-ridiculed Windows virtual assistant released by Microsoft in the 1990s, Gates notes that agents will be a real help. He sees them as beneficial in areas such as health care, education, productivity, entertainment, and shopping.

Gates wrote, "In short, agents will be able to help with virtually any activity and any area of life. The ramifications for the software business and for society will be profound."

This helps explain why another report estimates that by 2028 the market for agents will grow to nearly $29 billion. That's because agents will become an essential part of our daily, nonwork lives too.[68]

We're on the verge of things that would have sounded like science fiction not too long ago. Is it really that hard to imagine we'll have virtual assistants to help us with common tasks? I envision a day when a virtual assistant helps me when I run out of my favorite snack food. I'll be able to stand in my kitchen and say, "Hey, AI, I'm out of Oreos," and it knows the exact kind I like, how much I usually buy, and the snacks will just show up at my door within hours. There's nothing that stands in the way of that happening very soon.

Let's revisit *The Matrix* reference I made in Chapter 5 for a slightly different but still relevant point. It's the idea that we all need to wake up to the real world around us and realize that we're inevitably ceding ground to machines on fronts that would have been unimaginable even a few years ago. It absolutely is not a bad thing, either. Agents' abilities will be a welcomed development in our personal lives and businesses.

I always use one straightforward example to illustrate my point. It involves the nemesis of my business life.

The Dreaded Expense Report

"I do not like them, Sam-I-am."

Dr. Seuss had it right. Yes, expense reports are a necessary evil for every company. We need them for our basic business operations and accounting practices. But honestly, aren't they the worst things ever?

We all know from experience that they're hard enough to fill out correctly. But the approval process? It's maddening! What manager logs into work on a Monday morning and goes, "Sweet, there are 74 expense report approval requests in my inbox! I'm so excited to go click 'approve' over and over again!" Or even worse, something isn't filled out right, or not itemized, or lacks receipts. Then, you have to navigate an expense report app to figure out the problem.

Is this the best use of anyone's time? It's the opposite of efficiency. Hence, why I do not like them.

Today, expense report approval is a manual process because we need humans to provide judgment. Someone needs to review the report and make decisions based on knowledge of our company, policies, and ethics. It's interpretative. And yes, robotic processing automation can handle some of this. However, using software without AI is rigid and static. A human frequently has to address issues and exceptions. This is because you can't make a traditional expense report program with the number of if–then–else rules required for every possible exception and outcome. It would be crazy.

This is the current expense report process. Humans have to play a role, and there's a financial toll. One study found that the average business cost of processing one expense report is $58.[69] However, the days of the traditional approval process, as we know it, are numbered. I believe that within two years, no human will be needed to approve 99.9% of expense reports within a business. AI-powered agents will do it for you.

You will be able to create and train an agent using a pre-generative transformer that knows how to look at a receipt and make decisions based on your company policies and maybe 10,000 other expense reports that humans previously approved. Oh, and by the way, it will look for fraud. It will understand what "fraud" is without you having to create an infinite number of rules to explain it.

The agent will be able to reason, infer, and make judgments with a high probability of accuracy because it's based on an AI model grounded in all the information about your business. The agent can operate with some degree of ambiguity in ways that software without LLMs powering it cannot. The result will be agents approving expense reports faster and with more reliability.

What human would want to manually review and approve an expense report if it wasn't necessary? What company wouldn't view this as a more efficient process? I agree that expense reports are probably not the biggest time-wasting inconvenience that any of us face. But think about the hundreds if not thousands of other tedious tasks that people throughout your business must do every day. What are the efficiency gains if you eliminate those from their work routine?

This is what you need to get your arms around – *The Matrix* idea of waking up to our new reality. The humble expense report is just one small example of what's possible and coming. Dozens, hundreds, and even thousands of semi-autonomous and autonomous agents powered by AI models will be authorized to make decisions about your organization.

Agents will identify and act upon every type of data discovery imaginable. They will use software apps, websites, and other online tools, including spreadsheets, calendars, travel sites, and more. They will accomplish actions such as managing emails and setting up business meetings. (Have you ever had to schedule a Zoom call with six colleagues?) They will resolve common issues and handle inquiries in customer support, analyze data of all kinds, and personalize marketing campaigns. And on and on.

All of this, again, is possible because they can reason.

Agents will also learn and improve over time because they build upon themselves. AI can play a legitimate role whenever you believe human judgment is required. Agents will be trained with data from prior human actions. They will make rational decisions about your business at computer speed. Agents will be exponentially quicker, make fewer errors, and be smarter than humans in their specific domains.

Their use will also grow beyond everyday tasks. Those will just be the harbingers of the future. I envision a day when they optimize virtually everything in the software world. They will be able to improve your customer invoicing process, lead-to-opportunity marketing motion, supply chain processes, and so much more. We're going to see amazing things. It can make you dizzy just thinking about it. The possibilities are endless.

If I can play the role of a futurist for a moment, the day is not far off when the entirety of a company's operating system will be based on a large language model and agents. Maybe a business makes shirts. The model and its agent minions will orchestrate the process from start to finish. They will help you manufacture shirts more efficiently and at less cost. They will market the product and take orders. They will understand inventory in a way that recognizes when you have too many short-sleeved shirts in the warehouse, and winter's coming. So, the model will create, and agents will carry out, a sophisticated discount promotion on the website to move stock fast. And that will all just happen without human involvement.

We must think about how best to prepare for a world where that will be possible. You'll need to take steps now to leverage the power of agents. As they evolve, these highly sophisticated agents will require administration, observation, and supervision. This new business object requires a new kind of management.

Agent Management

When the Apple App Store opened in 2008, it had 500 applications you could download on your iPhone.[70] As of 2024, the number was approaching two million.[71] There are more than 2.6 million apps available for Android devices.[72] I predict that the coming explosion of agents won't be like what we observed with mobile device apps. The growth will far exceed it. As I mentioned in Chapter 1, there will be an Agent Economy.

This will inevitably lead to agent sprawl.

Your organization will have another business object within the architecture to manage and orchestrate, just like applications, databases, and APIs. And you will be accountable for the actions of these agents as part of your overall IT architecture. This is why businesses need to know what these agents are, who installed them, where they live, what they decide, their training methods, and whether they're hallucinating. Are they meeting governance requirements? What about standards around personally identifiable information? In other words, who is running the agent asylum?

I briefly mentioned in the data management chapter that with great power comes great responsibility. (Alert readers will recognize that I paraphrased the proverb Uncle Ben popularized in the Spider-Man movies when he gave that advice to Peter Parker.) This line bears repeating when we think about agents. They will be incredibly powerful, and it will be your responsibility to ensure that the power is helping your business and not hindering (or endangering) it.

Leaders need to know everything about agents because they are essentially digital employees that work for your company and represent you in the real world. Without management, mischief is possible, even if it's completely unintended. You'll need a fundamental understanding of everything about them.

Public marketplaces exist where anyone can find and download agents to accomplish specific tasks. If your organization is advanced in AI, you might already be building agents internally. I suspect those earlier adopters can figure out where I'm going here. You need a structured system to manage agents within your architecture.

Agent Registry

If you think of agent marketplaces as a version of the app store where you download the agents, the agent registry is your iPhone. It's the place in your architecture for containing agents. It's where all things agents happen and where you can keep tabs on them.

You will need this place to track and manage their activities. You will need an agent dashboard, activity logs, and runtime statuses. You will require a registry of every agent and comprehensive reports on what they're doing to ensure they're not running amok. It comes down to agent explainability. If these autonomous and semi-autonomous agents are tasked to do stuff, you need visibility into precisely how they do it.

I look at it from a CEO's perspective. I want to know what these agents have been approving, whether it's expense reports or something more significant. I'll use a hiring example that resonates with me because, as I mentioned before, I used to head a talent acquisition software company. Let's say my business has an agent helping us identify top job candidates based on their resumes. I need to know the selection criteria and ensure they match my company's values. But we can't do that without transparency into how that agent was trained and how it came to decisions. What, for instance, if it began to select candidates for interviews based on, say, a zip code preference? Talk about the opposite of diversity, equity, and inclusion! This isn't acceptable at any level.

You have to know everything about these agents, including if any biases somehow affect their choices. You want to be aware of every potential risk. So, it's not a stretch to think that monitoring the activities of agents will be mission-critical for your organization.

Teams of Agents

One of the big problems in these early days of AI is that the answers we get aren't always correct. AI wants to be helpful. So, when it doesn't know something, it can make up stuff just to have an answer. This is what we mean when we say it "hallucinates."

In some ways, we can think of AI as a young child. At a basic level, all a child wants to do is please their parents. If the child lacks information but knows the reward model will be making mom or dad happy, then they will invent something to do that. Similarly, AI will provide made-up answers when it doesn't have access to all the correct information – and do so with absolute confidence. But you can't have an unreliable narrator helping chart the course for your business.

The concern is that you will never get 100% accuracy with these large language models. That's a problem because, as we've discussed, 85% accuracy doesn't cut it when precision is crucial. Even 1% inaccuracy in something like health care can lead to terrible outcomes. So, how do we get around the hallucination problem?

My friend Dr. Vishal Sikka has thought a lot about this. There are few people I respect more than Vishal, and even fewer people understand AI better than he does. He's the former Chief Technology Officer for SAP and the Chief Executive Officer of Infosys. Today, he's the founder and CEO of Vianai Systems,[73] a company focused on using AI in a purposeful, human-centric, trusted way.

We've often discussed the difficulty of getting answers to relatively simple questions about our businesses. Vishal believes this is mainly due to the layers of technology built up over the years in the typical company's digital ecosystem, which results in a mountain of complexity. He believes the power of AI is the ability it gives us to talk directly to our systems, have real conversations, and quickly get answers – not just reports. The challenge is making sure those answers are correct.

"When you're dealing with financial numbers, you cannot be wrong," Vishal said during my company's 2024 user conference. "You cannot make mistakes. You cannot hallucinate. But hallucination is inherent to LLM technology itself. It's not easy to fix that because every company's data models and technologies are different. Mapping intent and transforming that in the right way to get the answers you want is a very hard problem to solve."

He believes agents – plural – are critical to the solution. A team of agents can circumvent the hallucination problem by acting together and double-checking their work.

Let's say you ask a chat agent: "Tell me the performance of this specific product over the last five quarters in these nine countries." The agent does its work to get the answer. But then, a second anti-hallucination agent checks the answer of the first agent. A third agent reports on any legal issues. A fourth accounting agent checks for compliance gap analysis. All these agents will work together in the background so that you get one fast response that's more reliable and trusted. You can even have agents powered by different models to tap into a greater range of capabilities, resulting in better performance.

If you think about it, humans already do this when consulting with colleagues from different departments to get answers. We work together. The medical industry has a name for this too. It's called second opinions.

I envision "agent swarms" working collaboratively to solve complex tasks. This coordination of agents explains why I firmly believe two things.

1. Agents will change our businesses.
2. There will be thousands of them within our organizations.

The Agentic Future

Every company on the planet is busy creating AI co-pilot experiences that you can talk to and help you do some things. That's all well and good. But it can't be just something that occasionally does stuff when asked. The power of agents is that they're always on, always working – without constant, hands-on management.

Now, there might be a sense of dread in the back of your mind when you think about the expansion of agents. What will this mean for jobs? My personal belief is that this doesn't mean jobs will go away. (It's a point I'll discuss at greater length in the upcoming chapter.) I think AI and agents will augment people, not replace them. For me, the formula is this idea:

Humans + Machines = Greater Success

You might already be familiar with the acronym HITL – which stands for "humans in the loop." It describes the critical role of people in providing oversight and context for AI.

We are better together. In our personal lives, everyone will have some kind of personal AI assistant – i.e., an agent. They'll be personalized to know who you are and remember your likes and preferences. They'll know enough about us and our jobs to remind us each morning: These are the three tasks you need to do today at work. From a business perspective, agents will improve over time, making our companies more efficient.

Within the context of your business, and specifically around integration, automation, data management, agents will be invented and introduced to you in the next few years to perform tasks bordering on magic. Cleaning your data autonomously, data discovery, and more.

However, agents will also increase your integration needs by orders of magnitude as they require connectivity with critical systems within your digital architecture. This is why you need an AI-driven integration and automation platform designed for your business to create interconnected and automated processes for applications, databases, APIs, and agents.

Agent Management: The AI Future Is Here

And there are specific things you should be looking for as you search for a platform that can make your organization more AI-ready. But before we discuss that, I want to share more from Dr. Vishal Sikka.

Chapter Takeaway

Three Things to Know

1. AI agents are software entities powered by AI models to perform tasks and make decisions independently within your organization.
2. Agents represent the next generation of AI that is only starting to impact how we work.
3. As agents expand exponentially throughout your business as they become more mainstream, you'll need a sophisticated way to manage their use.

Why It Matters

Agents have the potential to dramatically improve business efficiency and productivity while freeing people to work on more creative and impactful projects.

The Bottom Line

The agents aren't coming. They're already here. As their influence grows, your business will never be the same.

A Conversation with Dr. Vishal Sikka

■ ■ ■

Dr. Vishal Sikka doesn't mince words when he talks about the traditional experience of business users when they interact with technology systems at their organizations. "It's always been terrible," he said.

He believes AI is a massive opportunity to change this. The founder and CEO of Vianai Systems, Vishal is using AI to help people throughout the business have real conversations with their business operations. This enables them to finally get understandable and actionable answers, as opposed to reports and dashboards that can leave people struggling to parse out helpful insights.

I mentioned in the last chapter that Vishal is the former CTO for SAP and ran the IT consulting firm Infosys. A long-time student of AI and machine learning, he learned from John McCarthy and Marvin Minsky, two of the founding fathers of AI. A true visionary of the technology, Vishal frequently advises C-suite leaders on strategies for transforming their businesses.

Today, his Silicon Valley-based company is helping cut through the hype and show businesses how AI can provide real value. Perhaps what I find most impressive is how Vishal talks about AI. He spends less time focusing on the technology itself. Instead, he evangelizes the importance of using it responsibly in a purposeful, trusted, and human-centric way. He's someone we all should listen to regarding AI's potential and limitations.

> *Steve Lucas:* Vishal, I believe that all business software exists to create integrated and automated processes. I'm interested in your unique perspective because you're known as a leader who finds ways to get more from business processes.

Vishal Sikka: It's a very accurate assertion to say that's the whole point of computing technology. A business is a collection of people and systems, and it's a set of activities we perform between them. We research the potential buyers of products. We go through the process of making the products and bringing them to the customers. Then, we need to understand what was sold and do all the regulatory work around it. All these activities, processes, and tasks require making sure it gets done right, efficiently, cost-effectively, and fast. That's what technology has endeavored to enable for decades. That's why there's always been different degrees of automation and integration.

SL: Can you give an example of that evolution involving integrating systems and automation of processes?

VS: Think about the EKG. It used to be that you would have to go to a hospital because there were very few EKG machines. I grew up in a big city in India of maybe one million people. But in the entire town, there was just one EKG machine. Slowly, EKG machines began to show up in every clinic. Now, you can have an EKG on your watch. Here's a personal story. After I recovered from a case of COVID, I wasn't feeling well right before I needed to present at a board meeting. I called my doctor at Stanford, and he said, "Well, are you wearing your watch?" I did six EKGs in a row and sent him the results. And he said, "Oh, don't worry." We determined that I was suffering from a known COVID side effect from a sensitivity to drinking a glass of wine. But think about how marvelous it is to have that capability on your watch to read an EKG! That's a classic example of integration and automation. The app is not only integrated with the watch, but you

Digital Impact

can send it securely to a hospital system from the watch through an integration.

SL: That is an amazing, everyday example of how technology can improve our lives.

VS: We'll continue to see advances like that, as far as the eye can see, requiring different degrees of integration and automation. But my point is that digitization empowers people. It enables decision-making that's better, faster, cheaper, and more pervasive. The same thing has happened in enterprises in terms of financials, managing inventory, and being able to track things. My wife and I were recently tracking a package we had shipped to India from a different country. We knew exactly where it was, what was happening to it, who touched it, and all that. This kind of dramatic increase in granularity is the result of the digital work around data.

SL: As you think back over the past 30 years, have the integration and automation of processes reduced the number of humans in the loop and created more productivity as we use technology to create more iterative systems?

VS: Productivity has increased, and that's a good thing. If you look at the revenue per employee, it has gone up dramatically. That can be attributed to productivity gains enabled by technology. At the same time, my instinct is that the number of employees has not gone down because now employees can do more things than they did before. The amount of time it takes to respond to things and the amount of time it takes to come up with new things has shrunk dramatically. But it's not the same for all companies. That's why I think we see companies die a lot faster now. If you think about the Fortune 500 from 20 or even 10 years ago and compare it to today, it would be vastly different. It's shocking. These are the biggest companies in the world. You would think that they knew how to survive, outrun, defend, and adapt to change. But so many didn't.

SL: It's crazy how the road is littered with companies where the brand was amazing, but now it just doesn't exist. And it's not a Blockbuster Video cautionary tale. It's like thousands of companies.

VS: Yes! Thousands of companies!

SL: Then let me ask you some broader questions about how you think digital transformation fits into this. What did that phrase mean when you first heard it, and what do you believe it means today?

VS: My first encounter with that was a beautiful book Nicholas Negroponte wrote called *Being Digital*.[74] But digital transformation is basically how physical stuff, over time, disappears into software. All kinds of things get replaced. It's a steady and irrevocable process that's also exponential in nature. One way to think about it is by looking at music. The music players, LPs, and CDs are all largely gone. My dad used to be a photographer and had this darkroom upstairs at our house where he would process film. It was unbelievable to take these negatives, expose them to light on paper, and then process them chemically. Now, we can take an unlimited number of digital pictures. When things become digital, they become real time. They also become on the fly. From a business perspective, you don't have to wait for the imagination of some project manager to pre-build something for you. Or worry if a person deviates from what you wanted and has to reprogram things. All that goes away when you make things digital because it's immediately available.

SL: It's an exaggeration to say that all the paper is gone. But do you think there will be a time when digital transformation becomes irrelevant? Does digital transformation ever go away?

VS: Not for the foreseeable future. Things are going to continue to become more and more digitized. Just look around and think of all the physical things that still could be digitized.

SL: OK, when you think about all of the digital transformation conversations you've had in your career, were topics like integration and automation critical to those discussions? I often think people start with digital transformation by saying, "Well, we need this application." Where do they put questions like: "How are we going to get these things to talk to each other? How are we going to automate these processes?" My sense is it's not always at the forefront.

VS: The answer to that is the leading companies where digital transformation has succeeded always make integration and automation an integral part of their transformation. In cases where people say, "Oh, this is a job for technical people," the transformation is never good enough. It generally doesn't work without an emphasis on integrating systems and operational processes. That's a shocking thing for people. For any digital technology to work, the user has to understand what it is and what it can enable for them. If they don't understand it, then it doesn't work. Integration and automation are at the heart of it.

A Conversation with Dr. Vishal Sikka

SL: Shifting gears a bit, how do you think the future of digital transformation will change, specifically with AI? I guess what I'm really asking is why you created Vianai.

VS: Enterprises need reliable and trusted systems. They are not black boxes. My goal at Vianai was always to make a platform that made it possible for enterprises to build AI applications that were transparent and trusted and produced the right results. When ChatGPT happened, it was very clear that this hallucination problem was going to be the critical thing. That's the technical problem we're solving. But the business problem we're focused on goes back to your point about integration and automation. How do you make it possible for business users to get the information they want without having to rely on complex layers of IT people, third-party people, and systems that sit in between them and the information? A business leader wants to know what happened, what will happen, and what I do about it. Generative AI should make it easier to just talk to the system. But that's much harder than it seems because of the hallucination problem and the complexity of the meaning of requests. For instance, what does it really mean when you say, "What were my employee expenses last quarter," or, "Did I spend more on travel last quarter than the year before?" What year are you asking about? Is it the fiscal year? What quarter? What particular kinds of expenses? Then, you have the complexity of the underlying systems. We've solved that problem of making it possible for business users to get information from the underlying systems in real time by just talking to them. Of course, integration is essential because it connects all those systems.

SL: Many people I talk to believe that this generation of AI is overhyped. What do you think?

VS: It's both incredibly disruptive and overhyped. It's possible to believe both things simultaneously. It's overhyped because there are certain things it's incapable of doing, and people don't realize that. The hallucination problem will not just go away. It's fundamental to the nature of the technology. It's also not going to be technology that is the end of humanity or some other nonsense like robots shooting from the sky. On the other hand, it's incredibly powerful. Even a 20% productivity improvement is revolutionary. This will easily get us that, maybe up to 30%. But it needs to be contained. You need to put boundaries around it. You need to surround it in ways that make sure that the systems work in an accurate, trusted, and reliable way. It's a powerful tool with huge weaknesses. We also have to understand the limitations of the technology and work around those limitations.

SL: There's a lot to think about in that answer. Let me get a little more specific. How will AI change enterprise software in the next five years?

VS: To quote futurist William Gibson, "The future is already here – it is just not evenly distributed." The biggest impact I see on the enterprise software landscape is business users will be able to converse with their systems and data. They will type sentences in English or their native language and receive responses from systems and answers to what they seek. Soon after, they will converse with their systems with voice, feed pictures and live video feeds to their systems, and achieve significant productivity gains. This will require

A Conversation with Dr. Vishal Sikka

solving significant challenges and overcoming some huge barriers, such as privacy, understanding the user's intent, translating and mapping that intent to how underlying systems work, integrating securely into the underlying systems and data stores, and more.

SL: It feels like a brave new world with endless possibilities.

VS: We will see the development of new applications and new software systems. We will see the emergence of AI-enabled software development platforms and safe agentic architectures that enable development and execution in a fundamentally fluid and frictionless way. The adoption of AR and VR headsets will allow us to consume enterprise content in these paradigms too. Finally, AI will enable the inclusion of simulation, forecasting, and predictive capabilities into every activity people undertake. This will make it much easier for nontechnical business users to answer questions from large amounts of data, such as what happened, why did it happen, and what can we do about it. This sense-making at a large scale will make it easy for people to create thoughtful plans and strategies. In a nutshell, much easier access and development of enterprise systems will mean far higher productivity and agile business execution. So, strap on!

SL: I'm ready. And in 10 years?

VS: Over a 10-year horizon, I would add two additional things. One is personalization at scale. Our systems will have much deeper insights into who we are. They will have deep knowledge graphs of individual users and be true companions to us, helping us work and be better people. The second is quantum computing. The extreme computing needs AI will need to generate sustainably will help us finally reach the quantum computing era. I have been watching this for decades.

Now, I can finally see quantum deployment as a productive application at the top 1,000 companies by 2030 and widespread adoption of quantum in the enterprise by 2035.

Summary

What I love about my conversation with Vishal is how he seamlessly blends deep technical knowledge with a human-centric approach to AI. Vishal is a true visionary in the world of technology and certainly the AI space. He's worked with AI pioneers and brings a wealth of experience to the table. But what truly sets him apart is his focus on making AI not just a powerful tool but one that's accessible, transparent, and trustworthy.

Vishal's perspective on AI is refreshingly balanced. He acknowledges AI's immense potential to revolutionize business processes and decision-making. But he's also candid about its limitations – like the infamous "hallucination" problem in generative AI models. He's on a mission to ensure that AI serves people in an intuitive and understandable way, allowing business users to interact with their systems as naturally as they would with a human colleague.

Our discussion highlighted how AI could finally make business software more user-friendly, turning complex data into actionable insights without needing layers of technical interpretation. Vishal's vision is to strip away unnecessary complexity and make AI a tool that empowers people at every level of an organization. He's not just pushing for more AI. He's advocating for better, more responsible AI that truly benefits everyone.

Chapter 7

What You Need for AI-Driven Integration and Automation

What we discuss in this chapter:

- A new way of thinking is required to succeed in our AI future, and a new kind of connectivity and automation platform is needed.

- You need specific functionality requirements in an AI-driven integration and automation platform solution to set up your business for success. We explore 12 questions you should ask every connectivity vendor.

- How Tony's Chocolonely aligns business success with social justice by making delicious, exploitation-free chocolate.

"An impact company that happens to make chocolate."

Every bar of chocolate made by Tony's Chocolonely tells part of the company's story about its social justice mission.

It begins with the distinctive red wrapper on Tony's signature milk chocolate product, signaling a sense of alarm. Once opened, the chocolate pieces are separated in unequal sizes, symbolizing inequity in the cocoa industry supply chain. Some are in the shape of West African countries, where impoverished farmers grow about 60%

of the world's cocoa. Finally, the thick bar has a striking image of a broken chain. Together, they show the Dutch company's commitment to selling exploitation-free chocolate and ending the practice of child labor in cocoa production.

Tony's Chocolonely[75] isn't just in the business of selling tasty treats. It's leading a movement to ensure that an estimated 1.6 million children are no longer forced to toil on subsistence farms in Africa, where their families live in abject poverty.

Helped by global expansion, the fast-growing business recorded $162 million in revenue during the 2023 fiscal year. Perhaps even more significant is how it now supplies fair trade cocoa to other socially conscious companies and partners with brands like Ben & Jerry's through its Tony's Open Chain initiative, to play an ever-greater role in changing the world.[76]

"Tony's is doing something on a humanitarian basis," said Abhinav Gaur, a middleware specialist at Tony's Chocolonely. "We always say that we are not a chocolate company that makes an impact. We are an impact company that happens to make chocolates. This core value is evident everywhere in how people work at Tony's."

The company's origin story is extraordinary. In 2005, three Dutch journalists, including Teun van de Keuken, followed up their televised child labor exposé by launching a company where farmers would get a fair share of cocoa profits so that children could be in school, not working the fields in brutal conditions. Even the company name has a special meaning. *Teun* is the Dutch equivalent of Tony in English. And it indeed has been a lonely journey to be a values-led company in the chocolate industry.

The world, of course, loves chocolate. The United States alone spent more than $19 billion on the sweets in 2023.[77] However, the problems around child labor in cocoa production have been an open secret for decades. The leading chocolate manufacturers even signed a pledge in 2001 to eradicate what is essentially modern slavery, where young children wield machetes, carry heavy loads, and work with pesticides.[78] Instead, the problem grew.

Tony's Chocolonely is working to change that. The company is making a difference through the combination of delicious chocolate, brilliant marketing, and consumers' growing awareness of the ethical sourcing of the products they buy.

But changing the world also requires running a profitable business. Here's where the story turns to technology. Tony's Chocolonely ensures farmers finally get their fair share by running a cost-efficient business. This includes a lean technology team streamlining and automating processes, so less money is needed for back-office functions. This approach of showing other companies that they can be successful *and* be socially responsible is how Tony's Chocolonely rallies other businesses to its cause.

"We don't say that we are in competition with other brands because we want them to join us in our quest for fair trade and open chain," said Gaur, who manages integrations. "But profit is an essential part of the business. Otherwise, nobody will join your mission, even if you are doing good things for the world. Nobody will be convinced."

The Boomi Enterprise Platform has been an integral part of the company's expansion to eight countries, adding retailer sellers, opening brick-and-mortar stores, and powering a popular webshop featuring the ability to customize chocolate bars. The logistics of shipping products to partners and customers are daunting because they involve many different global systems that must connect and communicate seamlessly. This complexity only scales with more success.

"When you start a company, you have very few systems," Gaur said. "But as the company grows, the systems grow, and you outgrow the capacity to use point-to-point integrations. So, you need a system that can integrate everything. Integration has to be right in the center of the company so that all the systems can talk and synchronize with each other."

He added, "I'm not exaggerating when I say it would be nearly impossible for us to run a very big business without a core integration platform because every country is different. We could never replicate all the processes needed."

Gaur, a native of India who lives in the Netherlands, speaks four different languages and has a unique viewpoint on the cultural importance of connection. Just like people from different parts of the world might think their way of communicating is the best, technology systems think their "grammar" is also the best. Their programming insists that everything must align with their rules. However, that comes with conflict when two applications need to connect.

"That's where an integration platform comes in," Gaur said. "It allows both System A and System B to think they're deciding what grammar to use in their interaction by making sure it's correct for each one. But a good platform isn't just a translator because when you speak different languages, you also have different perspectives. It's like a brain between them that makes sure the different systems truly understand each other through information transformation."

Integration and automation help Tony's Chocolonely operate more efficiently and improve the lives of people in West Africa. As a bonus, chocolate lovers worldwide can enjoy their favorite treats with a clearer conscience.

"Most of us eat chocolates, and it's such a big part of our lives," Gaur said. "We never really give a thought about how it is made, and the people are making this chocolate possible for our celebrations. But when you realize what's happening, you have a different perspective. Chocolate should not just be our celebration. It should be a celebration for someone else too."

That's the sweet taste of success – and doing the right thing.

Key Points

- **Goal:** Ensure the business stays in high-growth mode during rapid expansion by using a modern technology backbone that creates more efficiencies in the global supply chain, while containing costs to ensure that a fair share of profits goes to cocoa farmers in West Africa.

- **Human Impact:** The Boomi Enterprise Platform is the connective tissue for the entire business, responsible for 200-plus integrations, including significant systems such as Salesforce and Microsoft Business Central, ecommerce platforms like Shopify, and a growing number of third-party logistics providers. The implementation time for new integrations was dramatically reduced from a month to as little as three days. This efficiency is crucial for the business to keep its promises of delivering chocolate products to retailers, partners, and consumers without unacceptable delays. For instance, when a large order is placed, it's processed automatically and confirmed for shipping with a logistics partner within seconds – with complete visibility.

- **Lessons Learned:** "Every system, probably just like every person, probably thinks that they are the smartest one in any conversation. But you need integration, sitting between them, smiling, and making their interactions work. So, that's my lesson learned. All systems and all humans are right in their own way. We just need that person or system in the middle to help them understand that no one is the smartest. We are just different, but we still need to communicate." – *Abhinav Gaur, Middleware Specialist, Tony's Chocolonely*

Addressing the Connectivity Problem

What could be a more worthy goal than striving to end child labor? Now that's an outcome with an impact. Tony's Chocolonely does it by making a connection that most of us probably never think about – linking our love for chocolate with how it's made. This is incredibly powerful.

There are several important takeaways from this story. One is the notion of doing as much good as possible. Every company has a mission statement. But I think it's fair to say that not nearly enough enshrine the idea of prioritizing a benefit for society as part of their vision. Tony's Chocolonely not only does this, but has also made it part of the value proposition to consumers.

It's more difficult for business-to-business (B2B) companies to do this, but not impossible. I have nothing but admiration for my former employer, Salesforce, and its brilliant CEO Marc Benioff.[79] The company has a "1-1-1 model" for committing 1% of its profits, technology, and employees' time to build a more equitable and sustainable world.[80] Doing as much good as possible is baked into the company's business philosophy.

A second insight involves digital transformation. When we think about modernization initiatives, we generally focus on things such as saved hours, faster transactions, fewer expenses, etc. There's nothing wrong with that, of course, because they all improve the health of our businesses. The lesson from Tony's Chocolonely is how those operational improvements ultimately benefit humans – specifically children. It's digital transformation with a purpose.

Finally, from a technology perspective, this story also vividly captures how success and growth become inextricably linked with more systems, applications, data, etc. It's always more, more, more. Abhinav Gaur gives a great explanation of how system fragmentation and complexity are impossible to avoid. It just happens. But Tony's

Chocolonely is also a great example of using connectivity to limit that complexity and create a more cohesive architecture that's also flexible enough to adapt and handle explosive expansion.

Throughout the book, we've been fleshing out the problems organizations have already been experiencing with digital transformation and why they will prevent your business from succeeding in the age of AI. I want to pause here to recap some of the key points we've discussed about connecting and simplifying a digital landscape for success today and in the future.

- Integration
- Data management
- Automation
- API management
- Agent management

Together, working collectively, they are the foundational pillars for maximizing the benefits of AI technology that's changing everything. So now, let's pull it all together and explain why it's so essential to have the capability to orchestrate all of these. I'm a visual person. Maybe you are too. I'm going to show you a series of images (Figures 7.1–7.5). Think of it as a book version of a whiteboard presentation. They illustrate how I think about the challenges every business faces today with complex digital architectures and the emerging need to incorporate AI into those landscapes.

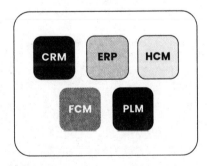

Figure 7.1 A few typical enterprise applications.

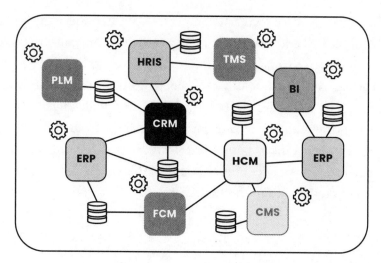

Figure 7.2 Gaining complexity with more apps and connections.

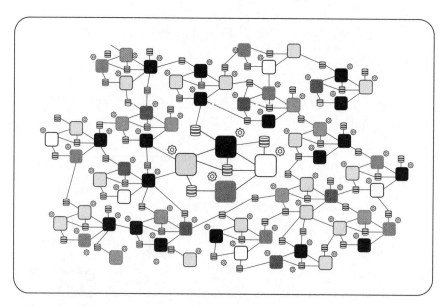

Figure 7.3 The typical enterprise landscape: digital sprawl.

Let's start with the most obvious part of any architecture – applications. I've included a few of the bedrock systems found in a typical enterprise, such as CRM, ERP, etc. But wouldn't it be terrific

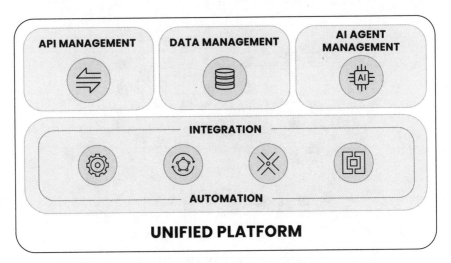

Figure 7.4 A unified platform to tame digital app sprawl.

to have only five platforms in your digital landscape? How easy life would be. You would probably be thinking: "Sweet!" But let's get a little closer to your reality.

As you can see, I've added other elements to the environment. We have databases containing essential information. Of course, we can't have everything sitting on islands. Things need to talk to each other, so you also have APIs to at least try to have interconnected processes. We're starting to get a little more complicated here. Still, this probably doesn't look like your tech stack yet.

This is more like it. I bet this image isn't too far off from the reality of your technology landscape – digital sprawl.

We've discussed how the typical enterprise has over 340 applications and countless databases and APIs that probably number in the thousands. But who knows for sure? You probably don't. All these data sources and critical systems, which were likely never designed to talk to one another in the first place, must be interconnected. If not, they're holding your business back. Even worse, AI will not work without connected systems and processes because it depends

What You Need for AI-Driven Integration and Automation

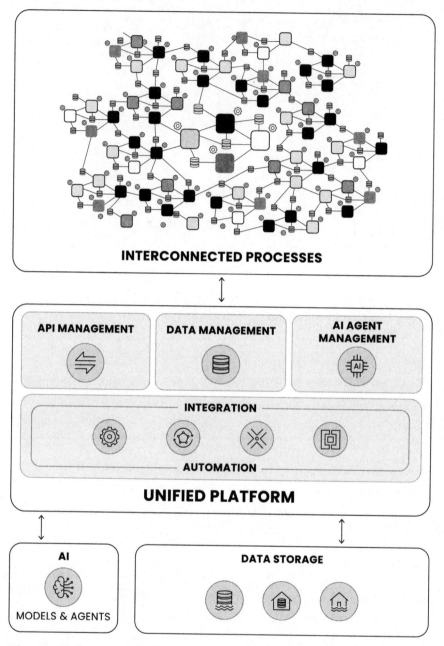

Figure 7.5 A unified platform powers and connects all your systems.

on the fuel of clean, accurate, and timely data. AI needs access to all these data sources to achieve the results you expect.

So, what's the answer?

If fragmentation is the fundamental problem in our disconnected technology environments, the answer to ending the chaos is a unified platform that connects and simplifies everything.

It's worth emphasizing once again. You need to identify "the one." Having multiple integration products won't solve your connectivity problems. This only creates another problem by forcing you to integrate integration solutions. If the goal is to simplify, why do you want multiple platforms to manage multiple integration processes? It adds more complexity and piles up more technical debt. The practical solution is to use a single, scalable platform to connect and manage your organization's critical business objects. It solves today's fragmentation problems and sets you up to make the most of AI. The platform sits at the heart of your digital environment and provides seamless connectivity for the entire organization.

We've discussed iPaaS – integration platform as a service – and how it became the widely accepted term for thinking about connectivity solutions. As a label, it probably was a pretty good descriptor of what businesses needed at one point. But you need to look behind the traditional idea of "iPaaS." You already know that I have deep misgivings about this acronym. In general, I dislike how we get caught in the trap of speaking in buzzwords and being acronym-compliant. This is particularly the case for iPaaS, which fails to capture the full breadth of what a modern connectivity solution needs to accomplish.

In business, we should always say what we mean in plain language. This includes the importance of connecting anything, anywhere, and at any time to create powerful outcomes. This is why I'm incredibly passionate about two terms that everyone can understand: integration and automation. I'll take it a step further.

What You Need for AI-Driven Integration and Automation

As AI becomes more indispensable to businesses, this is what you need to get the most from your technology architecture:

An AI-driven integration and automation platform.

It's central to modern digital architecture as it connects, automates, and simplifies your entire asset portfolio: applications, databases, data lakes and data warehouses, and APIs. And, coming to a business very near you, AI models and agents.

In other words, everything.

All the business objects within your architecture need to integrate through a single connectivity layer. Think of it as creating a "layer of abstraction" that provides flexible connectivity. This requires a holistic platform with Swiss army knife-like capabilities that can normalize all the digital assets in the organization into interoperable interfaces as opposed to just plugging System A together with System B. Imagine if all the appliances in your house had to be hardwired into some electrical power source. Instead, an AI-driven integration and automation platform is the universal plug that powers and connects all your systems.

By now, I hope I've persuaded you that a modern platform for orchestrating the integration of applications and automation of processes has become a must-have technology for business success in the age of AI. The larger business community certainly recognizes it. This technology category has been described as the fastest-growing segment in software. This also explains why so many solutions have jumped into the marketplace with lofty claims to solve problems caused by the lack of connectivity.

This is also why, as you explore platforms, your head will probably start spinning. It's like navigating a maze. There's a lot to take in, and it's easy to become overwhelmed and confused by pitches about features and explanations of capabilities. Eventually, every platform begins to sound similar. But they're not the same. At this point, you might wonder, "what should I look for in a platform, and what questions should I ask?"

I'm glad you brought that up. I have some thoughts.

What You Need in an AI-Driven Integration and Automation Platform

I'm sure you have plenty of experience evaluating software tools and deciding what Goldilocks platforms are "just right" for your organization. You know the standard questions regarding reliability, user support, customer references, etc. You know the actual price of any piece of software isn't the upfront cost but what it will take to maintain it over time. You're also probably a pro at assessing the long-term viability of a potential vendor.

Still, we can all use some help from time to time when we're shopping for something new. This includes when you're trying to decipher marketing jargon and determine whether a product's technical functionality is a good match for your business needs. As you perform your due diligence, I believe you need to identify specific attributes while exploring connectivity solutions. Information is power, and being a well informed consumer is essential as you search for the right solution for your organization.

Let's stick with car metaphors. You've walked into the AI-driven integration and automation platform showroom and are ready to kick the tires on connectivity solutions to find what best suits your business needs. Here are a dozen questions that I think you should ask about what's under the hood.

1. Can the platform connect hybrid architectures?

Today's digital world is about heterogeneous environments. Data is everywhere in modern architectures: data centers, in the cloud, on the edge. You have foundational systems such as ERPs, CRMs, and

HRIS platforms. You have countless applications of all kinds to solve specific problems. Their primary design and functionality aren't to talk to other systems and clouds.

Today, the CIO's primary job is to stitch all these varied technologies and data sources together so that information moves freely and securely. This means identifying a platform that can easily integrate cloud applications with one another, with a full spectrum of deployment options. Yet it also means connecting a cutting-edge solution to a critical mainframe that might date back to the last century yet is still an essential part of your digital architecture. And don't forget about the need to connect with countless IoT devices.

2. Is the platform independent?

This is incredibly important. You must have a flexible platform that's completely agnostic and will connect *everything to everything*. So, look for Switzerland. The platform must be a neutral party in the middle of your architecture that plays nicely with every business object across all endpoints. It shouldn't matter what vendor made an application. It must integrate with any other system you need to achieve your goals. Interoperability is the new coin of the digital realm.

This kind of platform is essential to avoid lock-in. You don't want any vendor dictating the structure of your business operations just because, for instance, SAP doesn't integrate easily with other non-SAP solutions. Businesses should serve their customers, not any specific business model. Independence enables you to run your organization as you see fit – and not be told how to do it.

3. Is the platform designed for everyone?

The days of IT developers doing all the heavy lifting around integration and automation are in the rear view mirror. Businesses that move fast and pivot quickly rely on democratization. That means giving the lines of business the ability to do their own work with minimal reliance on overwhelmed and understaffed IT teams. A user-friendly, low-code/no-code platform enables business professionals who don't have deep technical knowledge to integrate systems and automate workflows themselves. This platform model abstracts away the technical complexity of coding with a simplified, self-service portal where they can interact with the platform in a conversational user experience.

Giving business professionals the ability to configure, run/schedule, and monitor processes easily gives them greater ownership of their projects while eliminating the need for constant IT hand-holding. It's a win–win because business users can accomplish what they need faster, and the IT team can focus on work that requires their deep technical expertise.

4. How does the platform ensure trusted data?

A platform must have a centralized data hub that improves stewardship for discovery, governance, quality, consistency, and visibility while minimizing bias. Only with this kind of observability can you comprehensively monitor and understand the behavior of data within your architecture. It should provide the capability to create "a single source of truth" synchronized throughout all systems, so everyone can access the same trusted information. It needs event-streaming capabilities to stay current with any changes in your data.

I know that "Big Data" is a tired term. But the arrival of AI means our businesses will rely on even bigger data. You'll never get what you want from AI without a platform that helps you wrangle your proprietary data – lots and lots of data. So, the solution must quickly move trusted, real-time data at a large scale and volume, in and out of every conceivable source – with complete transparency. Without that 360-degree view of all the data within your business, you won't be AI-ready. Instead, data will be a liability for your organization.

5. Is the security enterprise-grade?

The sad fact is that bad actors are everywhere, and they want what's inside your business. As a CEO, I can tell you that's why I'm thinking about security every waking hour of every day. While functionality and reliability are always priorities in a connectivity platform, you'll also need to understand the features for moving that data safely, securely, and within regulatory compliance standards to all endpoints. Side note: The proverbial "single pane of glass" to monitor, manage, and control everything concerning your data also has the added benefit of providing better security.

Among the first questions I would ask: Can you show me security audits and certifications conducted by reputable, third-party compliance evaluators, such as FedRAMP, StateRAMP, SOC 1 and SOC 2, and HIPAA/HITECH?

6. What are the automation capabilities?

If integration is the action, then automation is the outcome. Make sure the platform allows for quickly building applications that strategically automate workflows to reduce tedious, manual tasks. Also, can you orchestrate processes through triggers, events, and other actions to get data where it's needed?

In addition to knowing how the platform handles system-to-system automation, find out how it enables the handoffs between systems and human work steps. And explore what kind of visibility it offers in terms of dashboards to identify and troubleshoot issues quickly.

7. What is the API functionality?

Of course, you need the platform to configure, deploy, and manage APIs to expose real-time integrations. But that's table stakes today. The key here is to determine if the platform has next-generation management capabilities that will serve you well in our increasingly API-centric world. API sprawl is real. Ensure the platform has control plane features with a federated approach to responsibly overseeing every API gateway in your ecosystem. IT needs vendor-agnostic administration of the entire lifecycle of every API within the business.

It should also give you a single view of all your APIs so that you can discover, audit, and manage them. Only then will you have the standardization and security needed for a comprehensive, scalable API strategy for the entire business. Finally, it should enable people without technical expertise to create value with them – another example of democratization in action.

8. What are the platform's composability capabilities?

The digital components you build should be reusable. (Remember the LEGOS® comparison?) The platform should enable modular design, so you can take what you've already designed and easily reassemble those core pieces into different applications and services. When you don't have to build everything from scratch each time, it will make your teams more efficient, push projects out the door faster, and allow your business to get more done.

Composability is one way to make IT a hero in the business. It allows technical leaders to say, "Yeah, we can meet that deadline," instead of carrying "The Department of No" label.

9. What does the platform do for trading partners?

Business is a team game, and electronic data interchange (EDI) is an unheralded workhorse of the global economy. EDI has been around for a long time, with its origins dating back to the famous Berlin Airlift.[81] There's nothing flashy about communicating critical business documents between companies in a standardized,

What You Need for AI-Driven Integration and Automation

digital format without human intervention. However, this dependable communication system between companies accounted for over 78% of all electronic business sales processed in 2019 alone. That translated to $7 trillion in sales.[82]

Because EDI will continue to be the lifeblood of business for the foreseeable future, with its importance firmly entrenched in supply chain networks, a platform must have robust capabilities to connect with all your partners and automate self-service interactions. It will also eliminate the expensive need for a separate EDI platform.

10. What is the partner ecosystem?

You can tell a lot about a vendor by the company it keeps. Does it have a deep partner bench? You want an integration and automation business that works with hundreds of technology partners – not just dozens – who are experts at helping clients get the most value from their technology investments.

Look for a vendor with strong alliances with the most established, best-in-class cloud providers, like Amazon Web Services (AWS), which specializes in premium service. Ask about their network of global systems integrators, who act as trusted advisors when helping clients create a holistic technology vision specific to their business that can accelerate business outcomes at scale. These strategic consultants prefer to work with only the best integration and automation platforms because they know it's the linchpin to their overall service by simplifying architectures. So, their endorsement of a platform carries weight.

11. Does the platform fuel social responsibility?

Any technology purchase is motivated by tangible business outcomes such as increased customer loyalty, brand differentiation, market competitiveness, and business value. However, you can also draw a straight line between those goals and running an organization that does its part to improve lives. Put another way, Business Impact + Social Responsibility = Greater Success.

When evaluating platforms and vendors, you'll ask for examples of traditional business gains: time and money savings, efficiencies, etc. But also, can the platform enable outcomes that contribute to a great corporate culture and make a broader difference? Think about the stories you've been reading throughout this book.

12. How does the platform both use and enable AI?

To get the most out of AI, there are two key platform requirements for integration and automation. Think of them as the different sides of the same coin.

First, there's the question of how the platform enables you to leverage AI. It should possess all the connectivity capabilities we've been discussing here, including:

- Integrating applications and data sources to connect to AI models
- Managing APIs that communicate with models and agents
- Enabling interoperability to automate processes

All that connectivity feeds data into the AI models to give them knowledge of your business processes. (In the next chapter, we'll explore this topic in more depth.) This enhances your ability to infuse AI into your business by orchestrating its use within processes. In other words, you're empowering AI capabilities.

Second, consider the AI functionality inside the platform. A survey by 451 Research found that 43% of respondents already use some form of AI-assisted integration platform and that 55% said AI is either "very important" or "important" for integrating data, applications, and processes.[83] You should look for a platform that uses AI to leverage de-identified metadata so that you can incorporate the knowledge of every developer and business user who came before you. It should automatically offer recommendations to accelerate integration and workflow creation – and learn from those interactions and the patterns to better guide your choices. The platform should have natural language AI capabilities that allow you to have prompt-driven conversations with your business.

It must also have capabilities to track, discover, and manage agents. (Remember, I told you that agent sprawl is coming.) It requires an agent architecture where you can train and ground them — think of this as being like a garden. This garden should also be pre-populated with agents that, for instance, can:

- Design integrations based on basic requests ("Connect Salesforce to NetSuite")
- Give practical suggestions for the next steps when building out integrations
- Answer questions asked in natural language
- Provide peace of mind around data privacy by protecting sensitive information
- Automatically write documentation for your integration processes

Finally, the platform should allow you to manage your own custom-built agents and agents from third parties.

Setting the Stage for Practical AI

I have some other advice about choosing any piece of software. Over the years, I've "kicked the tires" on more platforms, solutions, and tools than I recall. I've developed my evaluation checklist, which comes down to a few essential points that I think are useful when considering technology.

1. **Cost–Benefit:** In the software world, it's rare to see the benefit of something outweigh the cost. It happens maybe 20% of the time. Too often, I've seen businesses pursue major deployments or upgrades of foundational systems like ERPs for the sake of "It's going to get better" when what they have already works just fine.

2. **Time to Benefit:** Even if a platform perfectly fits my needs, it must show value as quickly as possible. We've all experienced frustrating implementations that seem to go on forever. The longer something takes to deploy, the less benefit you'll see.

3. **Impact on My Competitive Moat:** The technology needs to widen or deepen my competitive advantage (the moat) over rivals by improving market share or profitability through increasing brand recognition, creating better products, reducing costs, etc.

4. **Happy Customers:** I try to put myself in the shoes of end users, whether they are employees or customers, and determine if they will be pleased with a new solution. This has always made sense to me. Also, I prefer not to have angry people show up at my office door with pitchforks and torches.

All these items are important. Yet, looking at that list, number four stands out for me. Of course, functionality and cost ultimately are the reasons we make software purchase decisions. But I spend a lot of time thinking about how any platform impacts people. Will it help employees do their jobs more easily? Will it build richer relationships with partners? Will customers get and use your products and services with less frustration?

The best consumer companies – I think of Apple, Amazon, and Netflix – make it ridiculously simple for people to get what they want from their products. This convenience is a big part of their success. So, when looking for an integration and automation platform, determine which one will provide the optimal "easy button" experiences for your humans.

Remember this as you implement AI within your business. It will go a long way toward making AI more practical across your organization. But how long will it be before we begin to see real value from AI in our businesses? Paul Cormier, a true legend in software, has some thoughts about that.

Chapter Takeaway

Three Things to Know

1. Knowledge is power, especially when it's challenging to keep up with the fast-moving innovation in software.
2. Do your homework to identify one orchestration platform that best connects all business objects and data sources within your architecture.
3. Proceed cautiously with any integration and automation vendors that aren't sophisticated in how they help customers succeed with AI.

Why It Matters

Simplifying complex digital environments requires a platform that can create a single layer of connectivity throughout the entire organization and handle a variety of needs: integration, automation, data management, API management, and agent management.

The Bottom Line

There will always be many ways to solve any technology challenge. However, determining the best integration and automation platform to maximize AI for your business requires asking the right questions during the evaluation process.

A Conversation with Paul Cormier

■ ■ ■

Paul Cormier has left an indelible mark on the software world in one of the most impactful ways possible. He completely changed the dynamic of business by delivering the power of open source and community into the enterprise.

As the former CEO of Linux trailblazer Red Hat, Paul was the key driver of one of technology's most historic companies. During his 20-plus years with the company, he led Red Hat's enterprise subscription model and drove its open hybrid cloud strategy. It changed software forever. That work also proved instrumental in Red Hat's explosive growth and ultimate acquisition by IBM in 2019 for $34 billion.

He knows what it's like to be at the forefront of an emerging technology, which is why I believe he deserves to be mentioned in the same breath as leaders like Microsoft's Satya Nadella and Apple's Tim Cook.

Today, Paul is the chairperson emeritus at Red Hat and a senior operating partner at Francisco Partners. On a personal level, he's incredibly generous in sharing his guidance and wisdom whenever I'm mulling over a challenge or business decision. He's also the perfect business leader to have a thoughtful conversation about the realities of digital transformation and why it might take longer for organizations to see real value in AI – even as they rush to embrace the new technology.

Steve Lucas: Every business has been focused on digital transformation. What does it mean to you?

Paul Cormier: Well, you're not going to like this, but it's probably one of the biggest, most overused buzzwords out there.

SL: Actually, we're completely in agreement on that.

PC: I guess what it means to me is several things. In the earliest stage, it was simply everything moving from paper to digital. Then, there was the stage of moving everything online. That was followed by the stage of everything moving to mobile. None of this could have happened without the Internet because we now have everything at our fingertips. And it wouldn't have exploded nearly as far without mobile because, especially with the younger generations, we essentially have desktop computers in our hands. But as I think about your question, I guess there's a fourth stage. The cloud has made everything accessible no matter where you are in the world. Anyway, those stages are how I think about digital transformation. It's expanded enterprise computing because everything's gone digital, and the cloud has broken down the walls of the data centers. In some respects, the cloud is the new data center. Digital transformation has exploded all of that.

SL: Where do you see integration and automation fitting into transformation efforts at any business?

PC: Integration couldn't be more important or more needed than right now. Everything you have is spread across this virtual infrastructure. Your whole data center operation. All your applications. Everything. It's not so much physical within four walls anymore. So, when I say everything has gone digital, I mean everything is run by the applications. The applications are now the business. The people on the business side are funding the applications within an enterprise, so they're the ones driving the agenda. It's all become radically less centralized. I mean, it's like decentralization on steroids. Applications spread across internal data centers, multiple data centers, multiple clouds, and now all the way out to edge devices. We're at the point where we're all just trying to digest that, make it useful, efficient, cost-effective, and most importantly, secure. All four of those stages of digital transformation caused problems that needed to be solved, and that has been pushing technology forward.

SL: What would be one example of that?

PC: When we went from paper to digital, storage became a huge issue, right? That's one of the things that drove the cloud growth because now I can have endless storage. That reached the personal consumer level too. All my personal files aren't in a filing cabinet somewhere. They're in the cloud. We don't have photo albums because they're all online too.

SL: You're so right when you say that. There's a box in my basement where I put all my tax returns. It was frozen in time in 2009. That's the last time I put a printed copy of my tax return in the box. But let me bring us back to digital transformation. So many promises have been made that it would benefit organizations, but they haven't happened. What should companies be thinking about digital transformation now?

PC: I go back to my buzzword comment. Digital transformation is so overused. It's happened. It's still happening. It's changed our lives. But it's still a phrase with many disparate definitions and can turn people off. I think AI is risking the same

A Conversation with Paul Cormier

thing. It just means so many different things to so many people. You almost have to dig down a little to explain what you're talking about when you just say "AI."

SL: Hold that thought about AI for a moment. You've probably met with more CIOs than most human beings on the planet. What are some of the challenges that they're facing every day?

PC: I do know a lot of them. I would say that the CIO's biggest challenge today is "How do I tie all this stuff together and secure it?" That's what they're thinking about now. Or at least that's what they should be thinking. I know that's what their bosses, the CEOs, are thinking about. And as you know, CEOs can really be a pain.

SL: Yes, I have heard this.

PC: Today, everything is digital and application-based. The CIO's job has become, "How can I wrangle that all together because I'm the one responsible for doing it in an efficient, cost-effective way? Most importantly, I'm the one responsible for securing it." Now that everything is distributed, CIOs are the ones trying to pull it all back together. But the CIOs also are no longer holding all the cards.

SL: But most CIOs still own certain things related to security standards and governance, right?

PC: Absolutely. But making the rest of the company adhere to it is a different story. How many developers started out with the cloud using their own credit cards to get an AWS account? That kind of thing still happens, but only worse. If you get broken into by one of those security gaps, the CIO's job is on the line. So, yes, they're still accountable for it, which is why they're manic about pulling it all together. While they're responsible, the power largely has gone out to the endpoints in the business as organizations transform themselves. Still, it's up to the CIOs to integrate all the technologies the business wants.

SL: So then, where do integration and automation belong on the CIO's list of priorities?

PC: High. They fit together because when there's more integration, automation is necessary. If you're integrating four apps with each other, it's not very complex. But we're now integrating tens of thousands of apps and systems in disparate places across the world. That's a very deep integration problem, and you can't do that without automation because it doesn't scale. Or you would have to scale in terms of people to manage all the systems that can never seem to communicate effectively. That's why integration and automation go hand in hand.

SL: Without automation, there's a greater potential for mistakes, risks, and other failures.

PC: Think about this example. We sent a security push and found out a week later that it contained a worm. Now, you've got to know all the tens of thousands of places where it exists, bring it back, and then put out a new fix. Remember what I said about steroids? Think of the manual labor and the possibilities for human error when trying to solve for something like that. It's all because of the sprawl we've created, intended in a good way, in this highly distributed world.

SL: With AI, do you see it as a convergence, or even a capstone, of all the technologies that have come before it, like ubiquitous computing, GPUs, connectivity, and IoT?

A Conversation with Paul Cormier

PC: Absolutely, but we should also talk about open-source development. In some respects, it was a precursor to AI. When the world was closed source, you had one company deciding what would be built, what was good, and what was not good. They got to tell all of us that simply by distributing their software. Then, open source happened. Now you've got a whole bunch of different people who can show you better ideas, and you get to decide what's best for you. With AI, these models are learning, maturing, and deciding on the best path to take in an open way. That's why I say it's like open source.

SL: What role do you envision AI playing in the enterprise?

PC: The AI you're seeing today is by no means the end product. It's the prototype. For enterprises to really adopt this and consume AI to run their business better, they're going to have to integrate those public AI models with the proprietary pieces of knowledge in their businesses. How they secure those models with their proprietary data is the problem to solve when taking advantage of AI. Businesses need to trace back everything used to build that model – traceability, explainability – while safeguarding proprietary data that gives them a competitive advantage.

SL: Given that, how long do you think it takes businesses to start seeing a real material impact from AI?

PC: Three to five years. We always underestimate how long it will take to get these technologies into the real world and consume them. Think about it. You're an enterprise customer, but you're not an AI expert. It's like what happened with Linux. There weren't enough Linux engineers for every company to hire their own. It's going to be the same thing in

AI. It's about the skill level. It's going to be up to us, in the industry, to make it more consumable for non-AI experts.

SL: This may be the most obvious question, but should CEOs and CIOs invest in AI now, or should they wait and see how other businesses are faring?

PC: They absolutely should invest in it now. Every company should experiment with AI because the market is demanding it.

SL: And what happens if they don't?

PC: They're going to get left behind. But everyone will adopt AI, at least indirectly, because all products will have some level of AI built into them. The big companies that we all know about will get ahead sooner with AI because they'll have the resources. You'll see the fruits of AI in those companies earlier. It's all the other companies I'm talking about when I say it will take three to five years to find value.

SL: We've already seen thousands of AI models created. Companies are eagerly looking for ways to use those large language models. Within our businesses, autonomous agents will be doing more and more things. It sure seems like our architectures are getting more complex. What does the future hold for the world of integration and automation?

PC: The need certainly becomes greater. Enterprises need an easy button. The average enterprise can't do it all for themselves when it comes to consuming AI. That's why integration and automation will become even more powerful. I'm not sure it's accurate to say that every company will be an AI company. However, every company will use AI in its business to solve its problems.

SL: Paul, we are in violent agreement on that.

A Conversation with Paul Cormier

Summary

What I love about my conversation with Paul is how he brings a grounded perspective to the complexities of digital transformation and the evolving role of AI. Paul is a legend in the software world, having been a key figure in driving Red Hat's revolutionary open-source and hybrid cloud strategies, which ultimately led to the company's monumental acquisition by IBM. His insights into how the digital landscape has transformed – from moving data from paper to digital and to the current challenges of integrating and securing sprawling, decentralized systems – are invaluable.

Paul's pragmatic view on AI is particularly compelling. He acknowledges that while AI is immensely powerful, it's still in the prototype stage for enterprises. He emphasizes that businesses need to start experimenting with AI now. Still, they should be realistic about the timeline to see substantial benefits. His analogy comparing AI's development to that of Linux – where the availability of skilled professionals was a significant barrier – highlights the importance of making AI more consumable for nonexperts. This conversation is a reminder that while AI holds great promise, the road to realizing its full potential will require thoughtful integration, robust security, and a realistic approach to its adoption.

Chapter 8

A Framework for Practical AI

What we discuss in this chapter:

- Moving beyond the hype and finding practical business value from AI requires identifying tangible use cases, a willingness to experiment, and constantly measuring outcomes.

- Responsible use of AI goes beyond compliance and governance. It's about how AI impacts people.

- How Nature Fresh Farms implements AI in nearly every aspect of a sustainable growing process to improve the quality and yield of fruits and vegetables.

"We make a difference by growing things differently."

Nature Fresh Farms[84] is a vertically integrated greenhouse producer and marketer located in Ontario, Canada; Delta, Ohio; and Laredo, Texas. The business nurtures about 1.8 million plants year round in a controlled climate over 250 acres, producing peppers, cucumbers, tomatoes, and strawberries.

But that's not all the company grows.

"We're also growing data," said Keith Bradley, the company's Vice President of Information Technology. "We call it our green network."

That data enables the business to innovate with new technology to grow better, tastier produce more sustainably. "We like to say we make a difference by growing things differently," he added.

Artificial intelligence helps control everything in the plants' life-cycle, including providing optimal amounts of light, oxygen, water, and nutrient supplements, Bradley said. They measure everything from the amount of pruning a plant requires. The weight of vines. The length of time produce will stay fresh (on average) in customers' refrigerators. Nothing is left to chance. That means collecting and analyzing an astounding amount of raw information because each plant creates about 1.1 megabytes of stored data weekly.

"We record every possible metric to analyze the best-growing methods," Bradley explained. "How much was the yield? What was the quality? How did variables interact? At any given time, we might have five different systems monitoring each plant."

That's why a 15-foot-tall plant can grow more than 40 bell peppers in one season. The linchpin connecting it all is a connectivity platform that ensures that all the data from those AI-infused systems is properly aggregated, stored, standardized, and usable for analysis.

"For us, AI-readiness is providing more production from the same amount of acreage," Bradley said. "But it's not just about growing more produce. We're looking at how to make that produce taste better for consumers and last longer on the shelf. If you don't have data, it's not going to work. We've learned firsthand that you can have years and years of data, but if it's not in a usable state and accurate, then it's no good. It's actually even more of a hindrance because now you have to tell the AI what data to use and not use. But Boomi's integration platform has allowed us to trust that our data is in the right state to run artificial intelligence on top of it."

Nature Fresh Farms' AI-ready path began with a more traditional business use case: automating billing processes. The company ran on paper and spreadsheets. A cart was pushed from cubicle to cubicle with files for invoices, packing slips, etc. It would slowly make its way through the finance department, as employees would do their portion of the work order before it rolled on to the next person.

Bradley's team eliminated those manual tasks by implementing the Boomi Enterprise Platform. The antiquated system was replaced by a searchable database that became a single source of truth for all customer information. From that data hub, they created integration pipelines to take the right information to the right endpoints, such as the ERP, CRM, or invoice system – in the proper format for each system. Gone were the days of employees searching endlessly through file cabinets because something was stapled to the wrong piece of paper.

From there, much like fast-growing vines, the platform grew into the greenhouse.

While the back office might have needed updating, the growing operation was always state of the art. The company started in 1999 when mechanical engineer Peter Quiring, who had been building greenhouses for farmers, envisioned using technology to grow produce more efficiently. He launched Nature Fresh Farms, which has become one of Canada's largest independent greenhouse growers thanks to cutting-edge technology and a focus on sustainability.

"Back then, growers were manually opening and closing vents for sunlight," Bradley said. "He wanted a computer to control everything in the operation. In the years since, we've become a completely proactive greenhouse where everything is designed for steady, year-round growth."

This meant overcoming a big challenge. The different technology systems in the greenhouse didn't communicate well. The data they contained wasn't standardized. The integration platform changed that. It allows them to automatically create pipelines that feed a single repository of contextual, usable data. In other words, no more data silos in this farming operation. It also set the stage for introducing AI into the greenhouse.

One example is an AI imaging system that matches the colors of fruits and vegetables to ensure, for instance, that tomatoes in a single package are all the same shade of red. Using OpenVINO, a deep learning toolkit developed by Intel, Nature Fresh Farms can ensure that the vegetable is always at peak ripeness and that the product is eye-pleasing to the consumer.

This kind of technology is why people are always surprised by how much data they process. "Even my Dell Technologies rep couldn't figure out why in the world we were buying so many computers," Bradley said with a laugh. "He was like, 'You're a farm, right? What are you doing with all of this?'"

AI also plays a role in running a more sustainable farming operation. As the impact of climate change mounts around the globe, vegetable and fruit producers are increasingly heading indoors where they can control the growing conditions. Nature Fresh Farms takes a waste-not-want-not approach to lessen its environmental impact. Packing materials are compostable. A closed-loop system ensures the recycling of up to 98% of the water used in growing. One use of AI is optimizing energy use to maintain the best-growing temperature when burning recycled wood chips and natural gas. Then, the carbon dioxide by-product is funneled back into the greenhouse because it's a natural plant stimulant.

Not every AI experiment, of course, has been a success.

"We've had multiple failures in our AI journey," Bradley said. "We've learned, 'OK, this doesn't work. Let's look at this differently.'"

Nature Fresh Farms devised a plan to use AI-directed robot cameras to look for pests. Instead, Bradley said, it was a similar experience to searching for a pesky fly in your home: you never see it when looking for it.

"There are too many hiding spots under leaves that these bugs can live in," Bradley added. "The moment this robot makes noise coming through, it just flies away. So, we decided not to look for bugs hurting the plant and look for plants impacted by bugs. That's always a sure-tell sign where they are."

The organization is also considering how AI can help pollinate plants more efficiently. Right now, about 100,000 bumblebees do the job. But those industrious bees pollinate every flower when it might be healthier for the plant – and the yield – if only three-quarters were pollinated. Nature Fresh Farms is exploring whether AI can suggest ways to pollinate plants more efficiently.

"Eventually, everything will be AI-driven," Bradley added. "Master growers will be able to teach it new growing technologies. They will be like the Obi-Wan Kenobi Jedi masters teaching them to grow better."

Whatever comes next, Nature Fresh Farms knows that it has trusted data available to feed the AI engine that helps the company continue to produce the best fruits and vegetables.

Key Points

- **Goal:** Utilize AI to analyze vast amounts of data for decision-making so growers can optimize every aspect of the growing process to produce the best, most nutritious fruit and vegetables in an environmentally sustainable way.

- **Human Impact:** Nature Fresh Farms' infusion of AI into its growing strategy contributes to a yield between 8–10 times greater per meter squared than traditional farming. The business strives to increase its yield by 3–4% annually – double the typical standard.

- **Lessons Learned:** "The only way to succeed is by failing. We've done that many times. The biggest stigma with AI is thinking that when you're going down a path, you have to stick to it. We've learned that sometimes you have to destroy that path, go back to the data, and start rebuilding it in a new way. Don't be scared when it doesn't work the first time. Keep your vision of what you want to do, and you'll get there." – *Keith Bradley, Vice President of Information Technology, Nature Fresh Farms*

Embracing Practical AI

There's so much I love about this story. What's more impactful than finding innovative ways to grow healthful food? As the effects of climate change and population growth increase, Nature Fresh Farms is at the forefront of producing more with less. This example also touches upon two themes that mean a lot to me.

The first is curiosity. It's a trait I inherited from my father, who has a mechanical engineering degree and designed cooling systems for nuclear reactors, among many things. Now retired, he still takes university courses and carries a small notebook to jot down ideas and equations. (I have memories growing up where my mom would look over at my dad in church and see him with his head down, scribbling away. She would be furious that he wasn't paying attention.) I know that the "always learning" attitude is why I love building computers and tinkering with car engines.

Some of the best leaders I've ever worked for were also the most curious. The shortlist includes Bill McDermott,[85] who now is the CEO of ServiceNow, Adobe CEO Shantanu Narayen,[86] and Bernard Liautaud,[87] the founder of BusinessObjects. Although I've never worked for him, I'd put Microsoft's Satya Nadella[88] at the top of this list. He has talked often about his role in changing Microsoft's culture from a "know-it-all" state to a "learn-it-all" mentality.[89] What all these outstanding leaders have in common is they're always asking questions. They're always looking for different ways to solve problems. That same kind of curiosity and innovation drives Nature Fresh Farms.

The second is the concept of failure. I struggle with this word. You've never "failed" when you learn something that you can apply to another project. We've all heard the Thomas Edison quote, "I have not failed 10,000 times – I've successfully found 10,000 ways that will not work." Even one of history's most brilliant inventors experienced his fair share of failures.[90] Although I'm sure many of those missteps with the lightbulb were more about fine-tuning his invention until he thought it was commercially viable.

Maybe the better way to think about it is "failing well." When Keith Bradley talked about running into bumps with AI, he was smiling. The team simply tried a different approach. Maybe their first idea of using AI to track greenhouse pests didn't work. Instead, they found another way to address their problem by focusing on the targets (the plants) instead of the culprits (the insects).

As businesses embrace the AI era, there will be *a lot* of trial and error. We'll try things that don't work. We will have to reassess. We'll have to accept that failure – or whatever we call it – is part of progress. But we must have that culture and attitude of constantly testing and innovating.

We're already seeing how difficult that is in AI's early stages. The *Harvard Business Review* noted that organizations face serious roadblocks when implementing AI. HBR cited research showing that even as the vast majority (85%) are planning or already have deployed AI, nearly 42% lack confidence that their existing infrastructure is ready for the demands of artificial intelligence.[91]

Shawn Rogers, the CEO of the BARC research firm, conducted a study that produced strikingly similar results. He was the coauthor of a survey that found over 95% of respondents are currently addressing their plans for AI. However, only 20.5% could be characterized as being in a state of "High Readiness" for various reasons.[92]

"FOMO is real," Shawn said. "Everybody is afraid that they're going to miss this train, and that's understandable considering all the

A Framework for Practical AI

hype around AI. But the train has not left the station because the technology is not ready yet. But while you shouldn't feel like you're behind, you should be striving for a higher level of readiness, which means coming up with a good strategy around data, integration, and automation now."

Shawn touches on critical points I want to explore deeper. The hype around AI is enormous. Most organizations are not AI-ready. While adoption is still slow, it's gradually building speed as AI goes mainstream. Now is the time to lay the groundwork to make your organization successful in the future with practical AI use cases.

Everyone is trying to figure out how to implement AI correctly, scale it, and apply prudent governance to ensure we don't get lapped by competitors. Nobody wants to follow Blockbuster Video's foot-steps and fall behind the innovation curve. Now, I have nothing but fond memories of Blockbuster. It was a family ritual for us, finding a movie and getting microwave popcorn and Red Vines licorice. But times and technology change, and Blockbuster didn't. The company became irrelevant because it didn't adapt. At the same time, as we fast-forward to today and AI, there are still clear risks to consider when embracing the new technology.

My perspective is that success with AI hinges on tackling real, tangible business challenges – those pain points that have remained elusive or processes ripe for optimization. It's not about jumping on the AI bandwagon. It's about pinpointing high-impact, low-risk opportunities where AI can genuinely transform your operations. Low-hanging fruit use cases include:

- Identifying high-potential leads faster for sales and marketing
- Scheduling and routing deliveries within the supply chain
- Predicting and managing payments

- Summarizing processes and information

- Powering more intuitive chatbot experiences

AI needs to be useful. Consider a specific example we discussed in the automation chapter about helping a frontline salesperson become productive. What if a sales lead comes in, and AI automatically researches the person and news about the company? Then, it also writes an email outreach, a personalized note for LinkedIn, and prepares a phone call talk track. You've just saved the rep an hour of work. Now, when you can do that for 200 leads, that's potentially weeks of time savings the rep can put to other good uses.

This is profound. And this is the definition of practical AI.

AI-Readiness

It isn't a case of being either AI-ready or not. It's a spectrum. If you've been modernizing your business systems, getting your data house in order, and automating your processes, you're already ahead of the game in taking advantage of AI. The effort you've put into digital transformation has laid the groundwork. But there's still much to be done. AI-readiness is a journey that doesn't end at a particular destination.

My colleague Michael Bachman, known to many as just "Bachman," travels the world conducting workshops on practical AI. He leads small groups of C-level executives in whiteboard sessions where they think through what they want to achieve with AI. Bachman's aim is never to tell anyone what models to implement or how to use AI. Instead, he's a guide explaining what they need to consider to succeed in whatever AI journey they choose for their business.

Bachman developed what he calls the "Six Tenets of AI-Readiness." I want to share them here because they can be the foundation of a practical AI strategy within any business.

1. **Set Clear Goals:** Know what you want to do with AI. Establish realistic benchmarks that you can measure. That means clearly understanding what you can do with AI based on the constraints of your resources and investments. A significant first step is having the right vision and people to define, identify, and execute the processes needed to reach the desired outcomes.

2. **Know Your Processes:** Your business must catalog all the processes and workflows and deprecate unnecessary ones. If necessary processes don't yet exist, they will need to be created.

3. **Know Your Data:** AI's power to turn data into actionable outcomes is unprecedented. It's crucial to map what data you have, where it lives, why it's valuable, and how it's generated, refined, secured, and governed. Accessing, transforming, and moving data is what makes AI work. This includes system records, metadata, master data, reference data, labels, and logs.

4. **Align and Be Accountable:** Leaders and stakeholders should understand the expectations and work together as good stewards of data and processes. Of course, that's easier said than done, especially in large organizations. Getting everyone on the same page is crucial because AI requires orchestrating actions that stretch across the business. Holding everyone accountable increases your chances of creating a well-defined AI strategy for the entire organization.

5. **Prioritize Thoughtfully:** Establish a hierarchy of business core objectives, corporate values, and societal impact. Then, ensure the right balance between these priorities. Considerations can include complexity, risk, level of effort, internal versus external services, KPIs or OKRs, skill versus will, and responsible sustainability.

6. **Automate with Intention:** Transforming manual processes is essential to creating contextualized data pipelines that AI can use to produce outcomes. (More on that in a moment.) Implementing AI without understanding your processes or data will lead to inefficiencies, slow your business, and introduce risk.

If you demystify AI, it's really just a computational platform. AI is amazing because it operates at a speed and scale we've never seen. Still, the AI story is ultimately about data. How it's managed, accumulated, cataloged, channeled, secured, governed, restricted, and transformed. Bachman tells C-suite leaders in his workshops that it's essentially harnessing all the verbs you can apply to data.

While AI is a shiny new object, the stumbling blocks to making it practical have been staring us in the face forever. It comes back to the data "Vs" we discussed earlier in the book: volume, velocity, variety, veracity, and value. Everything that makes data "good" is a requirement to get the most from AI.

This brings us back to why integration and automation are so essential. If an AI model is the engine sitting at the heart of your business operations, it needs the fuel of high-quality data to run at its best. The idea of data pipelines in digital architectures is not new. But in the age of AI, the role of these pipelines is magnified.

Having the best large language model that's trained by vacuuming up vast data sets from the Internet is a good start. But it won't be able to answer your specific questions or perform every task you want because it doesn't know your business. It needs to be augmented with the private, proprietary data you hold dear and keep under lock and key.

It all comes down to context.

Creating Context for AI

Let's say you ask a colleague for help on a project. But you don't provide enough information about the task. What do you think the result will be? Probably not a good one. And it wouldn't be your coworker's fault, either. They didn't have everything needed to do the job correctly.

The same is true with AI. If you were to ask any publicly available AI model to create a more efficient marketing-to-sales handoff for high-quality leads within your business, you would get a perfectly acceptable, generic response about the steps any business should consider for optimizing the process. But it won't be particularly beneficial because it can't offer suggestions based on your business – let alone actually do it for you. It lacks insight into your systems, processes, and data. It's not "grounded" on your business.

The wave of emerging AI models is undoubtedly impressive. And each iteration is better than the last. But they only know what they're trained on – publicly available or licensed information. A generic model doesn't have access to *your* proprietary data. It's vanilla, and the information it contains is likely dated. That contributes to the problem of hallucinations because eager-to-please AI wants to provide some answer – reliable or not – even when it doesn't understand the proper context. The model, by itself, is not enough. However, you can increase the precision and accuracy of AI by fine-tuning the model with access to your proprietary data in applications so it can know everything about your business. It provides that vanilla model with the "flavoring" of data specifically about your business that is accurate and up to date.

This is why AI needs well-orchestrated data pipelines.

I defer again to Bachman for a moment because he literally co-wrote the book on this topic called *Modernizing Enterprise Data Pipelines*.[93] Specifically, as it relates to AI, Bachman explains that you now need "context pipelines" built for speed, scale, and security that feed the right data in the right form at the right time into a system of intelligence (AI). Data flows into a model from foundational systems such as CRMs, ERPs, inventory management systems, supply chain applications, data lakes/warehouses, etc. Then, once that information is transformed into usable insights by an AI model, it's delivered in "action pipelines" to the systems that ultimately get used to achieve outcomes (Figure 8.1).

Like, for instance, empowering agents.

Another dynamic technique that goes together with data pipelines is retrieval-augmented generation – RAG for short. We've briefly touched on RAG a couple of times already. It has become one of the cornerstones for thinking about AI more practically. It helps you get your hands on precise slices of data that can be infused into AI engines. RAG means what it says. You're enabling the model to *retrieve* bits of needed information that will help *augment* a

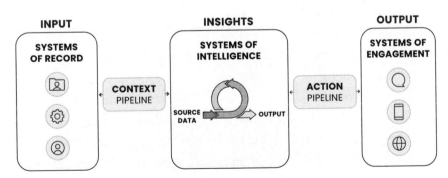

Figure 8.1 The AI-ready enterprise.

A Framework for Practical AI

generative AI process to improve the insights and actions it delivers. Fetching the most timely and relevant information on demand results in a more contextualized response or action to a specific query.

RAG is another way of helping AI models be as accurate as possible by giving them access to information they wouldn't otherwise have, like your sales and marketing information, customer service data, product innovation, financials, etc. You're helping AI help you by providing the model with trusted data. It automatically delivers subject-matter expertise, guiding the model to deliver better outcomes.

Enabling Actions

We're implementing AI into our businesses for one reason – to do stuff.

AI models are about language. Again, it's right there in the name: *large language models*. You give them words (questions), and they give you back words (answers). Or, in the case of the next level of intelligent automation – agents – you give them prompts, and they go right to work completing a wide range of objectives limited only by your imagination. Fraud detection. Predictive analysis. Workflow optimization. The applications are endless. (Don't forget about expense reports, either!) Agents are empowered to complete a range of tasks by giving them access to data and systems.

What makes this so exciting is the business can become a rocket ship when you've structured your processes to provide the AI engine with the proper fuel for takeoff.

Beyond completing simple tasks, AI can help with more comprehensive, big-picture planning when it knows your business. For instance, let's say you're a fast-growing company and need to ensure you're staffing the business appropriately in the right areas as you scale. You want to know how close you are to that traditional triangle shape with the proportion of fewer leaders at the top and more frontline workers at the base. You can ask an AI model to help you evaluate your organizational structure and suggest any possible changes.

That model will be trained on what businesses your size and industry typically look like in terms of employee levels. However, it can come back with specific insights and recommendations because it can access every part of your business through RAG functionality, such as HR data, the number of people within departments, etc. Maybe it delivers an answer that your company no longer resembles a traditional triangle, and there are staffing issues that you should consider addressing.

Why wouldn't you want the capability to use AI intuitively to help you make decisions and take action?

Responsible AI

People must be part of the process to ensure checks and balances on AI. This is why I've referred to the idea of "humans in the loop." They can implement practical guardrails that provide governance, security, and common sense. Nobody wants a dystopian movie to become a reality on their watch. Or, more realistically, no one wants AI to do something that reflects poorly on your company's reputation.

As you think about AI, it's critical to identify and manage possible risks and ensure the technology conforms with your business values. You need to consider everything that facilitates accountable deployment of AI. It's why my company chose to be part of the first-ever enterprise risk framework for generative artificial intelligence in collaboration with more than 1,000 leaders, academics, and industry bodies.[94] It's the right thing to do but also smart business. Companies want to work with other businesses that are thinking hard about the best ways to implement AI safely. How much human oversight of processes you'll want within your business ultimately comes down to your confidence level in letting AI act on your behalf.

But responsibility goes beyond compliance, governance, and regulatory concerns. AI will only be practical if it's transparent, bias-free, ethical, and truly helps people. It's never a mistake when you can align what's good for society with what's good for your business. You should think about the human experience for customers and employees. You'll use the technology responsibly if you do what's right for people. We shouldn't worry about AI becoming sentient because we're nowhere near that point. But all you have to do is look at these pictures of autonomous cars getting stuck in the middle of the road to understand the need for greater responsibility right now.

Believe me when I say that your employees are paying close attention to developments around AI. They care about their employer's views on the ethical use of AI and how it impacts them and society. The HBR article I cited earlier in this chapter raises an interesting point. It says: "Embracing an AI-first approach also sends a clear, subliminal message to employees, one that is not entirely motivating: if AI is first, they are at best second."[91] If I were to put it more bluntly, there's a lot of fear about jobs being outsourced to AI.

Historically, disruption is an inevitable result of wide-scale technological change. This includes how people work. It's safe to say that the shape of jobs will change with AI, which is something we'll have to confront as a society. For instance, people with jobs that involve repetitive, routine tasks that can easily be automated probably do have reason for concern. That said, don't count me among the doomsayers about negative impacts on the overall workforce. I'm in the AI optimist camp. It might not be a smooth transition in the short term, but I believe AI will create more jobs in the long run.

The Jevons Paradox isn't a perfect analogy to what's happening today with AI, but I think it's close. A nineteenth-century

English economist named William Stanley Jevons noted that when technological advances increased the efficiency of a resource – like coal – the subsequent demand for its use jumped rather than declined.[95] Yes, it's counterintuitive. However, lower costs and greater efficiency expanded the use of coal-burning engines to other kinds of machinery, ultimately increasing job opportunities.

I'm not an economist and won't play one in this book. However, there are parallels in the digital era. The cost of computing is remarkably cheaper today than it was 30 years ago. If you've noticed, efficiency hasn't exactly reduced jobs in the information age. It's just the opposite. Jobs certainly will change during the AI era. But I believe a new boom in AI-related skills is the most likely result.

Understandably, people are nervous about any technology they don't fully understand and worry that the ruthless efficiency of an unseen algorithm will cast them aside. Part of responsible AI is ensuring people are valued and understand they have a vital place in a workplace that embraces the technology. Robots aren't here to replace us – they're here to elevate us.

The explosion of AI tools offers a rare opportunity to reimagine how we work. If AI can take over three out of ten tasks in a workflow, it's not about reducing headcount. It's about amplifying human creativity and impact. The future isn't about humans versus machines. It's about humans and machines working in harmony. That's why companies should be transparent with their employees about the personal impact of business AI. It's important to foster a culture that embraces AI while ensuring employees feel valued and empowered. This includes reinforcing that collaboration between AI and humans provides opportunities for team members to focus on things that make a bigger difference to the organization – and are also more interesting to work on.

Bringing Practical AI to Life

AI has the potential to make a massive difference in healthcare, education, climate change, and so much more, including helping our businesses become more efficient and profitable. The challenge for all of us is turning that hype into reality.

AI is the number one topic for CEOs worldwide, which means it's also the top priority for IT teams. A late 2023 PwC Pulse Survey of Fortune 100 and private companies found that 84% of CIOs, CTOs, and technology leaders said they expect to use generative AI to support a new business model over the next 18 months.[96] Rarely have I seen a group of CIO-level technical leaders agree on a particular kind of technology as a high priority.

When I talk to my CEO peers, the concerns I hear are less about the safety of AI, the lack of regulation, or unforeseen consequences. What keeps them up at night is that someone else using AI will radically out-innovate them and their business model in the next 24–36 months. They don't know if there is a rival company out there that, thanks to AI, will leave them in the dust. So, they're eager to try new AI-infused solutions – at least in theory.

Reality, as we all know, is often different. According to the MIT Technology Review, just 5.4% of US businesses were using AI to produce a product or service in 2024.[97] We're all still in the very early stages of finding ways for AI to enhance our business processes.

At the same time, businesses are gearing up quickly. Today's leaders know they will ultimately be judged by the integrity of the AI models they build and implement. That's why organizations like yours are debating how to advance AI projects from pilot to production as fast as possible. Taking a crawl, walk, run approach to implementing AI within your organization is OK. You don't have to be the earliest of adopters. What's most important is that you're moving forward and gradually picking up speed.

But you need to get started. This requires an orchestrated framework of processes to support any AI model you choose to ensure it always has access to trusted, contextualized data. You must relentlessly focus on connecting and automating everything in your business. When you do this, great things are possible.

Chapter Takeaway

Three Things to Know

1. AI will be practical for your business only when you identify clear use cases and can measure the results to show business value.
2. Infusing proprietary data about your business into a model to produce desired outcomes will require creating context and action pipelines.
3. Taking a responsible approach to AI means staying true to your values, implementing safeguards, and being transparent with people about potential impacts.

Why It Matters

Solving the fundamental problems that every business faces today around data management – discovery, enrichment, validation, synchronization, and transport – is crucial to implementing practical use cases with AI.

The Bottom Line

There is no guarantee that you will succeed if you invest in AI. But there is a guarantee you will fail if you don't invest in AI.

Chapter 9

Building Your Digital Impact Mission

What we discuss in this chapter:

- The AI revolution is not being overhyped. It's being under-hyped.

- Succeeding at digital transformation is about more than just creating business efficiencies. It's about lasting, positive change in people's lives.

- How Cornell University has created a connected campus by enabling the integration of systems and automation of processes for the prestigious college with a global reach.

"We've discovered strength in simplicity."

Whenever a student or member of the faculty and staff does something at Cornell University, an unseen integration between digital systems is likely helping to make it happen: for example, processing a visit to the healthcare center, eating at a dining hall, entering an athletic facility, riding a campus bus, attending a Zoom call, and accessing course lists.

Connecting digital systems using APIs with an AI-driven integration and automation platform enables these activities and many more – all happening behind the scenes.

"Most people don't even realize our integration platform is in the picture, operating quietly in the background and connecting everything," said John Parker, a Cornell Information Technologies (CIT) software engineer/systems architect. "It's ubiquitous. It's everywhere. And it's a little bit of a secret."

Cornell, an Ivy League university that currently boasts 52 Nobel Laureates, is located in the picturesque city of Ithaca in the Finger Lakes region of upstate New York. The world-renowned university's reach stretches to every county in the state and worldwide, with campuses and programs in New York City, the Middle East, Europe, and beyond.[98]

It's a mammoth task to keep more than 27,000 students and 20,000 faculty and staff digitally connected to what they need. That's why CIT is working hard to transform its digital operations.

In the 1990s, the university's technical operations centered around a large, on-premises data center. Adding applications required one-off integrations to the mainframe that required endless lines of coding by hand. That changed as the CIT group led the migration to systems such as Workday and PeopleSoft, which could be hosted in the cloud – and were, incidentally, co-founded by a Cornell graduate.

However, in its digital transformation journey, Cornell's CIT team found that shifting foundational systems to the cloud and keeping them connected within a hybrid architecture was a heavy lift – beyond the capabilities of traditional middleware solutions. To eliminate the "spaghetti code," they implemented a series of integration platforms, finally settling on the Boomi Enterprise Platform.

"At first, I thought Boomi was too simple to do what we needed," Parker said. "But we've discovered strength in that simplicity."

Parker added that even if most people on campus don't realize the impact of systems integration on their daily lives, the central IT team appreciates the platform's role as the connective thread between Workday, PeopleSoft, Salesforce, identity management, finance systems, the endowment account management system, and a growing number of downstream applications. Today, many critical Cornell systems are in the cloud, and the platform sits between several of them.

An example of the power of enabling "citizen development" was an integration to connect the university with the endowment account management system. That demonstrated the simplicity of development on the platform as a summer intern learned to work with Boomi and solve the need in just five weeks.

For Parker, the innovative projects using API-enabled integration that improve daily lives, many of which are dreamed up and executed by students, are an integral part of the excitement of working at Cornell. One example is a research project by the university's Division of Nutritional Sciences, an effort that aims to gather and analyze parental food choices by inviting them to email photos of what they serve their children at home.

"Projects like that are why integration is a game-changer," Parker added.

Key Points

- **Goal:** Eliminating the friction from the everyday lives of students, faculty, and staff by connecting systems, so everyone can focus on the mission of maintaining a world-class educational and research institution.

- **Human Impact:** Dozens of systems across a hybrid environment of cloud applications are connected, including foundational applications such as SAP Concur, Blackboard, and Kuali Financial System. Jeff Christen, the CIT manager for data warehousing and integrations, also teaches a popular combined graduate/undergraduate-level course where students can gain practical knowledge in solving and enhancing real-world business problems that involve connecting digital architectures.[99]

- **Lessons Learned:** "Our team gets excited about mastering data. But we've learned that it's really hard to find a way to match data in ways that will satisfy the needs and goals of different parties. Everyone thinks, 'My data is my data, and that's exactly the way I want it.' My advice is to get your arms around your data and decide what you want and can do before you get started. You've got to understand what you're building before you pick up the hammer." – *John Parker, Cornell Information Technologies software engineer/systems architect*

The Power of Envisioning Success

Ending child labor in the growing of cocoa beans; ensuring cancer patients get to their life-saving treatments; helping families stay financially secure; delivering trusted health information during a global pandemic; finding innovative ways to provide consumers with nutritious fruits, vegetables, and juices; providing a world-class education; and assisting people after a natural disaster and ensuring their golden years are enjoyable.

It's a privilege to share these stories and others about organizations doing extraordinary things. Are you feeling inspired? I know I am. It's incredible how they each identified a worthwhile mission people could rally around and worked to bring that vision to life. Connected technology plays a pivotal role in helping these leaders achieve these great things. But in each case, the journey started with an idea.

I mentioned that when I first joined Boomi, I was in "absorb" mode. It's something I've learned to do as a new CEO of a company. I try not to assume anything. Then, after I have a firm grasp of the business, our people, the market, competitors, and so on, I take a step back and do something else.

Daydream.

When we call someone a "daydreamer," it's often intended as a gentle slight about how that person is frivolous or always has their head stuck in the clouds. They're not as serious or "down to earth" as we feel they should be. But I believe daydreaming can be powerful. It's a way to envision the world as we would like it to be. I'll think, "If the stars align and we accomplish everything possible at our company, what would that look like? What would the media headline be for our business? What will people say about us?"

Or, put another way, what would winning look like? Of course, dreams are different from goals. Execution and focus are how we bring success to life. But you first need that vision of winning.

That's a philosophy preached by ServiceNow CEO Bill McDermott. I consider Bill a mentor and someone who perhaps gave me the most valuable piece of business advice I've ever received. Earlier in my career, I once told him of my aspirations to someday become a CEO and my concern that I might not have the requisite qualities. In his distinctive New York accent, Bill told me, "Steve, you be you." It was his way of saying I should be a first-rate version of myself and not a second-rate version of somebody else. Years later, it's something that I've never forgotten.

Another thing I always remember about Bill is his fervent belief in a simple concept: People like to win. Bill even titled his best-selling memoir, *Winners Dream*.[100] Nobody likes to lose, even though there are valuable lessons to learn from setbacks. But let's be honest. People enjoy being part of accomplished organizations that others admire. I don't think it's shallow either. This is the formula for success. Talent gravitates toward talent, launching a virtuous cycle where it becomes possible for high-performing, like-minded people to create something unique.

None of this is rocket science. But I want to note it because the organizations detailed here also know something else. Yes, people want to work for successful businesses. But they also want to feel like their work matters and that they are doing something to make the world a better place. Do you know who else notices? Consumers. A study commissioned by Google Cloud showed that 82% of shoppers look for brands with values that align with their own – and this is where they spend their money.[101]

A business can be healthy and profitable, a market leader, please investors, employ many people, *and* make an impact. Doing great things by putting people first ought to be a goal for all of us. There's no reason your business can't make a real difference. You can be part of the connectivity that changes the world.

We're All in This Life Together

I firmly believe in another proverb. If you want to go fast, go alone. But if you want to go far, go together.

This has certainly been the case in my business career. It constantly amazes me how many people show up and care. I wouldn't be where I am today without the help of others, and there's no way I could pull off the whole CEO thing on a daily basis without a fantastic support system.

The same holds true in my personal life. I always say that it's not just me managing my Type 1 diabetes. It's the people around me. My wife Shelley watches over me like a hawk. I mean it in a literal sense when I say that I wouldn't be here today without her. It's the same with our two amazing children, who are now young adults. I've lost count of the times one of them has told me: "Dad, is your blood sugar low? Are you feeling OK?" My family is my rock.

I know how fortunate I am. This is why our family pays it forward. I've been a board member of the American Diabetes

Association. Shelley and I are involved with the Children's Diabetes Foundation and the University of Colorado's Barbara Davis Center for Diabetes, which provides care for kids from families who can't afford it.[102] We've also funded an Endowed Chair position at the University of Colorado Hospital to further the search for a cure for diabetes. The proceeds of this book will go to the University of Colorado Hospital to support its efforts to improve the lives of thousands of people.

I also try to be as transparent as possible about my experiences with diabetes because it might help someone else who is going through a tough time. I was lucky that the onset of my Type 1 didn't happen until later in life. I was already an adult, which made coping with the lifestyle changes much easier. (Although Shelley often teases me that it was so appropriate that I was diagnosed with what's also known as *juvenile* diabetes.)

There's nothing funny about children or teenagers getting this genetic condition. It's so much harder for them, and they shouldn't have to deal with it. It forces them to grow up too quickly.

This is why I make time to connect with young people who are struggling and don't see the point of managing their diabetes. I share with them my story and how what I initially thought was a curse turned out to be a blessing. I tell them there's so much they can achieve despite what they might perceive as limitations. The condition can even make them better people. Nothing makes me happier than showing them the possibilities of a full, healthy, and productive life. I'm a living example of that.

My hope is that we'll eradicate this disease in my lifetime. In the meantime, I'm spreading awareness about how technological innovations can dramatically improve a person's quality of life. I believe we're on the cusp of giant leaps forward in treating diabetes and other chronic illnesses – likely with the help of AI.

Building Your Digital Impact Mission

Now that you know my personal story, you can also see that it's no accident that I lead a company with a deep-rooted philosophy that connecting technology can help people.

With that, I will end where I began.

The Power of Connection

The term "digital transformation" has not aged well. Many people – maybe even you – have become understandably jaded about its intent, perhaps thinking it's just a marketing catchphrase software companies use to sell more stuff that you probably don't need.

The reality is less nefarious. There's a great paradox to modernization. While cutting-edge technologies can solve many existing problems, they also create new ones. The resulting complexity often drains away the benefits of innovation. Still, the goals of digitally transforming operations remain essential for business success. When you can simplify your processes by integrating pivotal systems and data, your business will run more efficiently. Your employees will be more productive. Promises will be kept to customers. You'll be more competitive in the marketplace.

Of course, if that were easy, you wouldn't have read this book. Lack of connectivity has always been a challenge. The resulting digital fragmentation acts as a kryptonite that foils modernization efforts.

But now you know that it doesn't have to be that way. You've seen how you can replace fragmentation with cohesion. We've explored what other organizations are achieving and how they're executing strategically to make their dreams and aspirations a reality. You can do the same thing.

Perhaps your business isn't directly doing something as dramatic as some examples highlighted in this book. But don't sell yourself short. Every organization today isn't just selling products and services.

They're selling experiences. Whatever your business does, its helping people solve problems or enjoy their lives more.

The harsh reality is that you have no choice but to embrace digital cohesion. You no longer have the luxury of thinking about integration and automation as "nice to have" capabilities for your business. Viewing connectivity as "just" an IT infrastructure challenge will doom your business to irrelevance in the age of AI. Today, every company must experiment with ways to leverage AI to its advantage, scale it, and profit from it – all while exercising careful governance over it. Ignoring the potential to enhance and augment your business processes is a fool's errand.

But achieving this potential requires making your business AI-ready. That will only happen with seamless connectivity and automated processes. This is how you can succeed at digital transformation, accelerate AI innovation, and impact the world. It's not about "outcomes." It's about creating a lasting, positive change.

Making a difference and success go hand in hand. The stories you've read about fantastic companies, nonprofits, government agencies, and universities were possible because all these organizations created connected digital architectures that put them in a position to do these wonderful things. They understood the need to orchestrate and maintain the most efficient processes possible to help their people do their best work. This is why they designed connectivity strategies and then implemented a modern platform for orchestrating today's critical business objects: applications, databases, and APIs. They're also well-positioned to take advantage of the coming emphasis on the newest element, AI agents.

Digital transformation doesn't will itself into existence, and neither will AI. It's not even about technology. It's the people who will always bring something into existence. They are the crucial "input" for any transformation project. As former Deloitte CIO Larry Quinlan

Building Your Digital Impact Mission

explained, thinking about the "output" – how something impacts people – is the difference maker. The most important thing is to ask yourself: "How will this initiative make life easier for the actual people who have to use it?" And once the change happens, do we ask them if they actually like it?"

When I started this book, my goal was for readers to learn something. I genuinely hope you have, because I learned a lot during this process. For example, Larry made me reflect when he talked about what we should consider success in digital transformation. Looking back, I can think of maybe a thousand ways in my career where I was part of a project that I thought would benefit someone. But I'm still not sure I paused often enough and asked people if it transformed their experiences as anticipated. We all have ideas, but do we take the time to find out if they work? We're often fixated on concepts like "product-market fit" and probably glossing over whether our projects truly benefited humans.

That's the essence of digital impact and the true definition of digital transformation. If it fails to help humans, what is the point? It all comes back to people and connection. Our businesses are better when all the systems, processes, and data within the enterprise are connected. The world is a better place when we're connected.

My Invitation to You

Criticism of the tech community has become fashionable. I understand why so many are deeply suspicious of technology. They've seen a Silicon Valley ethos of "move fast and break things" that too often leaves things broken – to the great detriment of society. These concerns go a long way to explaining some of the wariness we now see around AI.

A measurable portion of society no longer trusts the tech community to innovate safely or do the right thing. One 2024 study even found that including "AI" on product labels might drive away consumers, not entice them.[103] You can't blame people for being skeptical of what they don't yet understand. In tech terms, they see AI as disruptive – a bug, not a feature.

But I am an optimist. Technology can disrupt in positive ways too. When harnessed properly, AI will unlock fantastic opportunities for our businesses and the world. I feel privileged to have a platform to discuss something that I believe will radically change everything.

So many amazing things are happening. We're just beginning to see the first swell of this next great wave of technology evolution. This will be the most productive decade to come in the history of humankind. That's why I sometimes think that I was born in the wrong year. I wish I were just starting my career and had another 30 or 40 years to help bring AI-driven innovation to life. I envy younger people who have the opportunity to take enterprise software to the next level and do great things with this technology.

Is this AI Big Bang moment overhyped? I believe that it's under-hyped. We can't yet comprehend where the ability of technology to emulate human thinking will take us. But it will affect every aspect of our lives. How we think of software and what it does for our businesses will be completely rewritten. Things that we thought, even a year ago, were implausible are becoming achievable. The gap between potential and value is closing. The future is bright with the promise of innovation.

The crucial question is whether we're ready to seize the opportunity. It's about rising to the challenge and being prepared to take advantage of this technology. Companies that lack a strategy for connectivity will be replaced by those that have embraced one. But with a relentless focus on integration and automation, your business will be well-prepared to join the winners and can make a memorable impact.

Every story starts with a connection.

So, what story will you tell to help change the world?

Author Bio

Steve Lucas is the Chairman and Chief Executive Officer of Boomi, a global leader in intelligent integration and automation. With nearly three decades of technology experience shaping the enterprise software landscape, Steve has led transformational growth as CEO of Marketo and iCIMS and held pivotal leadership roles at industry giants such as Salesforce, SAP, Adobe, and more. A passionate advocate for innovation and impact, Steve also dedicates his expertise to philanthropy, having served on boards like the American Diabetes Association and the Children's Diabetes Foundation. He resides in Colorado with his family, balancing his professional pursuits with a commitment to making a difference.

About Boomi

Boomi, the AI-driven integration and automation platform, helps organizations around the world automate and streamline critical processes to achieve business outcomes faster. Harnessing advanced AI capabilities, the Boomi Enterprise Platform seamlessly connects systems and manages data flows with API management, integration, data management, and AI orchestration in one comprehensive solution. With a customer base exceeding 23,000 companies globally and a rapidly expanding network of 800+ partners, Boomi is revolutionizing the way enterprises of all sizes achieve business agility and operational excellence. Discover more at boomi.com.

Acknowledgments

It takes a village to write a book, and I'm indebted to the people who worked so hard to help me make this happen. Mark Emmons and Danalynne Menegus, thank you for your passion and dedication in helping make this book a reality! Just to mention a few more folks involved in making this book a success: Betsy Atkins, Michael Bachman, Rahim Bhatia, Alison Biggan, David Bobrowski, Keith Bradley, Nikki Chesworth, Jeff Christen, Paul Cormier, Emily Danis, Tom Davenport, Jasmine Ee, Mark Fields, Nicole Fishers, Abhinav Gaur, Barry Gerdsen, Diana Hancock, Jacob Hoffman, Laura Jackson, Ricky Koch, Jeff Lischett, Ed Macosky, Ann Maya, Matt McLarty, Megan McQuail, Patricia Moore, Mandy Nerone, Meghan Noel, John Parker, Frank Provenzano, Larry Quinlan, Shawn Rogers, Mitch Rosenbaum, Jaime Ryan, Kaitlin Ryan, Josh Rutberg, Waseem Samaan, Babita Savitsky, Dr. Vishal Sikka, Dinesh Singh, Delia Vallejo, R "Ray" Wang, Sean Wechter, and Brett Wilson.

Notes

a. CRM Magazine. "Meet the New ROI for AI Projects: Return on Transformation Investment (RTI)," July 5, 2024. https://www.destinationcrm.com/Articles/Columns-Departments/Customer-Experience/Meet-the-New-ROI-for-AI-Projects-Return-on-Transformation-Investment-(RTI)-164826.aspx.

1. Arthur Charles Clarke. *Profiles of the Future: An Inquiry into the Limits of the Possible*. n.d. https://www.amazon.com/Profiles-Future-Inquiry-Limits-Possible/dp/0575402776.

2. Kai McKeever Bullard et al. "Prevalence of Diagnosed Diabetes in Adults by Diabetes Type—United States, 2016," Morbidity and Mortality Weekly Report 67, no. 12 (March 30, 2018): 359–361, https://doi.org/10.15585/mmwr.mm6712a2.

3. Boomi. "Boomi Integration Platform as a Service: Connect Everything," July 8, 2024, https://boomi.com/.

4. "Engage to Win: A Blueprint for Success in the Engagement Economy. n.d. https://www.amazon.com/Engage-Win-Blueprint-Success-Engagement/dp/1626344981.

5. "Home," Australian Red Cross, n.d., https://www.redcross.org.au/.

6. Amy Lyall. "Big donations, famous faces and an incredible amount raised for Australia Unites: Red Cross Flood Appeal 2022," nine.com.au, March, 13, 2022, https://www.nine.com.au/entertainment/latest/australia-unites-red-cross-flood-appeal-2022-money-raised-performances-celebrities-wrap-up/6cfe92bf-b2e9-4b51-ad72-d71120771f27.

7. "An Active Social Life May Help You Live Longer," News, May 14, 2019, https://www.hsph.harvard.edu/news/hsph-in-the-news/active-social-life-longevity/.

8. Jared Spataro. "2 Years of Digital Transformation in 2 Months," Microsoft 365 Blog, June 29, 2022, https://www.microsoft.com/en-us/microsoft-365/blog/2020/04/30/2-years-digital-transformation-2-months/.

9. Okta. "Businesses at Work 2024," 2024, https://www.okta.com/sites/default/files/2024-04/Okta-2024_Businesses_at_Work.pdf.

10. Productiv. "State of SaaS—Productiv," May 3, 2024, https://productiv.com/state-of-saas-trends/.

11. Informatica. "Informatica Unveils 2021 State of the CDO Study," December 20, 2021, "Informatica Unveils 2021 State of the CDO Study," December 20, 2021. https://www.informatica.com/about-us/news/news-releases/2021/12/20211209-informatica-unveils-2021-state-of-the-cdo-study.html.

12. Eric Lamarre. "The Value of Digital Transformation," Harvard Business Review, August 1, 2023, https://hbr.org/2023/07/the-value-of-digital-transformation.

13. "Three New Mandates for Capturing a Digital Transformation's Full Value," McKinsey & Company, June 15, 2022, https://www.mckinsey.com/capabilities/mckinsey-digital/our-insights/three-new-mandates-for-capturing-a-digital-transformations-full-value.

14. Boomi. "Independent Study by Boomi Links Wasted Cloud Spend to Blind Cost Management Strategies—Boomi," Boomi Resources, April 2, 2024, https://resources.boomi.com/resources/resources-library/cloud-spend-study.

15. Gerrit De Vynck. "The AI Hype Bubble Is Deflating. Now Comes the Hard Part," Washington Post, April 27, 2024, https://www.washingtonpost.com/technology/2024/04/18/ai-bubble-hype-dying-money/.

16. "AI Investment Forecast to Approach $200 Billion Globally by 2025," Goldman Sachs, August 1, 2023, https://www.goldmansachs.com/intelligence/pages/ai-investment-forecast-to-approach-200-billion-globally-by-2025.html.

17. "Microsoft, OpenAI plan $100 billion data-center project," Reuters, March 29, 2024, https://www.reuters.com/technology/microsoft-openai-planning-100-billion-data-center-project-information-reports-2024-03-29/.

18. Mickle, Tripp. "Nvidia Revenue Jumps 122% in Positive Sign for Tech's A.I. Boom." *New York Times*, August 28, 2024. https://www.nytimes.com/2024/08/28/technology/nvidia-earnings-ai-stocks.html.

19. "What Matters Most? Eight CEO Priorities for 2024," McKinsey & Company, December 12, 2023, https://www.mckinsey.com/capabilities/strategy-and-corporate-finance/our-insights/what-matters-most-eight-ceo-priorities-for-2024.

20. PricewaterhouseCoopers. "Thriving in an Age of Continuous Reinvention," PwC, n.d., https://www.pwc.com/gx/en/issues/c-suite-insights/ceo-survey.html.

21. Wikipedia contributors. "Skynet (Terminator)," Wikipedia, May 10, 2024, https://en.wikipedia.org/wiki/Skynet_(Terminator).

22. Simmone Shah. "Sam Altman on OpenAI, Future Risks and Rewards, and Artificial General Intelligence," TIME, December 13, 2023, https://time.com/6344160/a-year-in-time-ceo-interview-sam-altman/.

23. Jay Mathews. "Half of the World Is Bilingual. What's Our Problem?," Washington Post, April 25, 2019, https://www.washingtonpost.com/local/education/half-the-world-is-bilingual-whats-our-problem/2019/04/24/1c2b0cc2-6625-11e9-a1b6-b29b90efa879_story.html.

24. Keith Guttridge, Andrew Comes, Shrey Pasricha, Max van den Berk, and Andrew Humphreys. "Gartner®, Magic Quadrant for Integration Platform as a Service," February 19, 2024, https://www.gartner.com/en/documents/5198963.

25. American Cancer Society. "Information and Resources About Cancer: Breast, Colon, Lung, Prostate, Skin," n.d. https://www.cancer.org/.

26. American Cancer Society. "Lifetime Risk of Developing or Dying from Cancer," https://www.cancer.org/cancer/risk-prevention/understanding-cancer-risk/lifetime-probability-of-developing-or-dying-from-cancer.html.

27. Give.org | BBB Wise Giving Alliance. "American Cancer Society Charity Review & Reports by Give.org," n.d. https://give.org/charity-reviews/Health/American-Cancer-Society-in-Kennesaw-ga-186.

28. Tim Faith, Denis Torii, and Paul Schenck. "The Future of ERP is Composable," Gartner, October 13, 2020, https://www.gartner.com/document/3991664.

29. Scott Brinker. "2024 Marketing Technology Landscape Supergraphic—14,106 Martech Products (27.8% Growth YoY)," Chief Marketing Technologist, May 7, 2024, https://chiefmartec.com/2024/05/2024-marketing-technology-landscape-supergraphic-14106-martech-products-27-8-growth-yoy/.

30. Boomi. "The EDI Buyer's Guide for Modern Supply Chain," March 22, 2024, https://boomi.com/content/guide/the-edi-buyers-guide/.

31. Steve Lucas. "How to Supercharge Companies—Advice From a Car Buff and 3-Time CEO," March 15, 2024, https://www.linkedin.com/pulse/how-supercharge-companies-advice-from-car-buff-3-time-steve-lucas-hl5hf/?trackingId=IFU%2F3ZbKTEz4HyIVEk8Nnw%3D%3D.

32. "From 2010 to 2019, Data Flows Among Countries Increased at a 45% Annual Rate. Digital Fragmentation Risks That Progress. #Wef24," World Economic Forum, January 11, 2024, https://www.weforum.org/agenda/2024/01/digital-fragmentation-risks-harming-cybersecurity-curtailing-ai/.

33. Boomi. "Forrester Wave iPaaS, 2023—Boomi," February 5, 2024, https://boomi.com/content/report/forrester-wave/.

34. Boomi. "Forrester Study | Cloud Costs Are Out of Control: Integration and Modernization Rein Them In," March 14, 2024, https://boomi.com/content/report/forrester-study-cloud-costs-integration-savings/.

35. "NCDHHS: North Carolina Department of Health and Human Services," n.d., https://www.ncdhhs.gov/.

36. Angelica Peebles. "One U.S. State's Laser Focus on Data Helps Shrink Racial Vaccine Gap," Bloomberg, March 6, 2021, https://www.bloomberg.com/news/articles/2021-03-06/one-u-s-state-s-laser-focus-on-data-helps-shrink-racial-vaccine-gap.

37. Boomi. "North Carolina Department of Health and Human Services Recognized as StateScoop 50 Winner." July 8, 2021, https://resources.boomi.com/resources/resources-library/north-carolina-department-of-health-and-human-services-recognized-as-statescoop-50-winner.

38. Ben Lutkevich and Ivy Wigmore. "3 V's (Volume, Velocity and Variety)," WhatIs, March 3, 2023, https://www.techtarget.com/whatis/definition/3Vs.

39. The Economist. "The World's Most Valuable Resource Is No Longer Oil, but Data," The Economist, May 6, 2017, https://www.economist.com/leaders/2017/05/06/the-worlds-most-valuable-resource-is-no-longer-oil-but-data.

40. "Amazon.com: Unbundling the Enterprise: APIs, Optionality, and the Science of Happy Accidents, n.d. https://www.amazon.com/Unbundling-Enterprise-Innovation-Optionality-Accidents/dp/1950508870.

41. "Secrets to a Successful AI Strategy," Constellation Research Inc., April 12, 2024, https://www.constellationr.com/research/secrets-successful-ai-strategy.

42. *All-in on AI: How Smart Companies Win Big with Artificial Intelligence*: Davenport, Thomas H., Mittal, Nitin, Pages 88–89, 9781647824693, n.d. https://www.amazon.com/All-AI-Companies-Artificial-Intelligence/dp/1647824699.

43. Suffolk Construction. "Suffolk Construction | USA Company & Building Services," Suffolk Construction, March 8, 2024, https://www.suffolk.com/.

44. Kalyra. "Kalyra—It's Different Here | Retirement Living, Aged Care and Help at Home," March 22, 2023. https://kalyra.org.au/.

45. Flinders University. "Flinders University—Adelaide, South Australia," n.d. https://www.flinders.edu.au/.

46. Adobe, Shantanu Narayen, Chair and Chief Executive Officer, https://www.adobe.com/about-adobe/leaders/shantanu-narayen.html.

47. Hasso Plattner Foundation, "Founder – Hasso Plattner Foundation," March 26, 2024, https://plattnerfoundation.org/hasso-plattner/.

48. "Larry Ellison | Executive Biography," n.d. https://www.oracle.com/corporate/executives/larry-ellison/.

49. Wikipedia contributors. "J.A.R.V.I.S." Wikipedia, May 27, 2024. https://en.wikipedia.org/wiki/J.A.R.V.I.S.

50. "Be Board Ready: The Secrets to Landing a Board Seat and Being a Great Director, n.d. https://www.amazon.com/Be-Board-Ready-Secrets-Director/dp/1949709337.

51. Constellation Research Inc. "13 Artificial Intelligence Takeaways From Constellation Research's AI," September 29, 2024. https://www.constellationr.com/blog-news/insights/13-artificial-intelligence-takeaways-constellation-research-s-ai-forum.

52. Business Wire. "IDC Spending Guide Sees Worldwide Digital Transformation Investments Reaching $3.4 Trillion in 2026," October 26, 2022. https://www.businesswire.com/news/home/20221026005193/en/IDC-Spending-Guide-Sees-Worldwide-Digital-Transformation-Investments-Reaching-3.4-Trillion-in-2026.

53. https://www.cuofco.org/.

54. National Credit Union Administration Quarterly Credit Union Data Summary 2022 Q4, https://ncua.gov/files/publications/analysis/quarterly-data-summary-2022-Q4.pdf.

55. Boomi. "Credit Union of Colorado Sees NPS Scores Leap 5% with Boomi-Powered Digital Member Experiences, https://resources.boomi.com/resources/resources-library/case-study-credit-union-of-colorado.

56. Imperva. "The State of API Security in 2024," April 3, 2024, https://www.imperva.com/resources/resource-library/reports/the-state-of-api-security-in-2024/.

57. "The API Experience Podcast," Boomi Podcasts—Boomi, December 11, 2023. https://boomi.com/boomi-podcasts/.

58. "Unbundling the Enterprise: APIs, Optionality, and the Science of Happy Accidents," Pages 147–150, n.d. https://www.amazon.com/Unbundling-Enterprise-Innovation-Optionality-Accidents/dp/1950508870.

59. "API and Integration Data Overview: Forrester's Developer Survey, 2023 | Forrester," Forrester, n.d., https://www.forrester.com/report/api-and-integration-data-overview-forresters-developer-survey-2023/RES180062.

60. Prasanth Aby Thomas. "A Third of Web Attacks Targeted APIs in 2023, Threatening the Expanding API Economy," *CSO Online*, March 19, 2024, https://www.csoonline.com/article/2066789/a-third-of-web-attacks-targeted-apis-in-2023-threatening-the-expanding-api-economy.html.

61. Jessica Marie. "The 2023 State of API Security Report—Global Findings," Traceable API Security, September 22, 2023, https://traceable.ai/2023-state-of-api-security.

62. "Tropicana Brands Group—Reinventing the Future of Juice," n.d., https://www.tropicanabrandsgroup.com/.

63. Steven Levy, "8 Google Employees Invented Modern AI. Here's the Inside Story," WIRED, March 20, 2024, https://www.wired.com/story/eight-google-employees-invented-modern-ai-transformers-paper/.

64. Capgemini Research Institute. "Harnessing the Value of Generative AI: 2nd Edition Top Uses Cases Across Sectors," 2024, https://www.capgemini.com/wp-content/uploads/2024/07/Generative-AI-in-Organizations-Refresh.pdf.

65. Gartner. "Gartner Predicts One-Third of Interactions with GenAI Services Will Use Action Models & Autonomous Agents for Task Completion by 2028," March 11, 2024, https://www.gartner.com/en/newsroom/press-releases/2024-03-11-gartner-predicts-one-third-of-interactions-with-genai-services-will-use-action-models-and-autonomous-agents-for-task-completion-by-2028.

66. Constellation Research Inc. "Boomi CEO Lucas: AI Agents Will Outnumber Your Human Employees Soon," September 23, 2024. https://www.constellationr.com/blog-news/insights/boomi-ceo-lucas-ai-agents-will-outnumber-your-human-employees-soon.

67. Bill Gates. "AI Is About to Completely Change How You Use Computers," *Gatesnotes.Com*, November 9, 2023, https://www.gatesnotes.com/AI-agents.

Notes

68. MarketsandMarkets. "Autonomous AI and Autonomous Agents Market Share, Forecast | Growth Analysis by 2030," n.d. https://www.markets andmarkets.com/Market-Reports/autonomous-ai-and-autonomous-agents-market-208190735.html.

69. "How Much Do Expense Reports Really Cost a Company?—Global Business Travel Association—GBTA," Global Business Travel Association—GBTA, July 20, 2022, https://www.gbta.org/how-much-do-expense-reports-really-cost-a-company/.

70. Apple. "The App Store Turns 10," *Apple Newsroom*, May 16, 2024, https://www.apple.com/newsroom/2018/07/app-store-turns-10/.

71. "App Store Data (2024)—Business of Apps," Business of Apps, January 23, 2024, https://www.businessofapps.com/data/app-stores/.

72. "Google Play Store Statistics (2024)—Business of Apps," February 6, 2024. https://www.businessofapps.com/data/google-play-statistics/.

73. Viani, n.d., https://www.vian.ai/.

74. Negroponte, Nicholas, and Marty Asher. Being Digital, 1995. https://en.wikipedia.org/wiki/Being_Digital.

75. https://tonyschocolonely.com/us/en.

76. License Global. "Tony's Chocolonely x Ben & Jerry's New Chocolate Bars and Ice Cream," February 1, 2023, https://www.licenseglobal.com/food-beverages/tony-s-chocolonely-x-ben-jerry-s-new-chocolate-bars-and-ice-cream.

77. CBS News. "Will the soaring price of cocoa turn chocolate into a luxury item?" April 2, 2024, https://www.cbsnews.com/news/chocolate-cocoa-hershey-candy/.

78. Washington Post. "U.S. report: "Much of the world's chocolate supply relies on more than 1 million child workers," October 18, 2020, https://www.washingtonpost.com/business/2020/10/19/million-child-laborers-chocolate-supply/.

79. "Marc Benioff Bio," Salesforce, n.d., https://www.salesforce.com/company/marc-benioff-bio/.

80. Salesforce. "Our Founders Created the 1% Pledge.," n.d. https://www.salesforce.com/company/pledge/.

81. "Milestones in the History of U.S. Foreign Relations—Office of the Historian," n.d. https://history.state.gov/milestones/1945-1952/berlin-airlift.

82. Brohan, Mark. "Why EDI Still Has a Big Role to Play in B2B Ecommerce." Digital Commerce 360, August 14, 2020. https://www.digital commerce360.com/2020/06/01/why-edi-still-has-a-big-role-to-play-in-b2b-ecommerce/.

83. Boomi. "The Impact of AI on Enterprise Integration and Automation | 451 Research," May 16, 2024, https://boomi.com/content/ebook/impact-of-ai-451-research/.

84. Nature Fresh Farms. "Home | Nature Fresh Farms," Nature Fresh Farms, December 5, 2023, https://www.naturefresh.ca/.

85. "Bill McDermott—ServiceNow," ServiceNow, n.d., https://www.service now.com/company/leadership/bill-mcdermott.html.

86. Adobe. Shantanu Narayen, Chair and Chief Executive Officer, https://www.adobe.com/about-adobe/leaders/shantanu-narayen.html.

87. Balderton Capital. "Bernard Liautaud | Balderton Capital," Balderton Capital—Leading Venture Firm Focused on Early and Early Growth Stage Investments in European Founded Companies, May 23, 2024, https://www.balderton.com/team/bernard-liautaud/.

88. "Satya Nadella—Stories," Stories, June 4, 2024, https://news.microsoft.com/exec/satya-nadella/.

89. Inc. "Satya Nadella's Microsoft Just Became the Most Valued Company in the World. And It's Thanks to Psychology, Not Tech." January 16, 2024, https://www.inc.com/nick-hobson/satya-nadellas-microsoft-just-became-most-valued-company-in-world-its-thanks-to-psychology-not-tech.html.

90. Smithsonian Magazine. "7 Epic Fails Brought to You By the Genius Mind of Thomas Edison," November 20, 2013, https://www.smithsonianmag.com/innovation/7-epic-fails-brought-to-you-by-the-genius-mind-of-thomas-edison-180947786/.

91. Oguz A. Acar. "Is Your AI-First Strategy Causing More Problems Than It's Solving?," Harvard Business Review, March 18, 2024, https://hbr.org/2024/03/is-your-ai-first-strategy-causing-more-problems-than-its-solving.

92. Boomi, "BARC | Optimizing Your Architecture for AI Innovation," May 16, 2024, https://boomi.com/content/report/barc-survey-ai-architecture-boomi/.

93. "Modern Enterprise Data Pipelines—Boomi," June 25, 2021. https://boomi.com/content/ebook/modern-enterprise-data-pipelines/.

94. "AI Governance Framework," n.d., https://www.genai.global/home.

95. Wikipedia contributors. "Jevons Paradox," Wikipedia, July 6, 2024, https://en.wikipedia.org/wiki/Jevons_paradox.

96. PricewaterhouseCoopers. "Technology Leader Insights From the PwC Pulse Survey," PwC, n.d., https://www.pwc.com/us/en/library/pulse-survey/business-reinvention/technology-leaders.html.

97. MIT Technology Review. "A Playbook for Crafting AI Strategy." *MIT Technology Review*, August 5, 2024. https://www.technologyreview.com/2024/08/05/1095447/a-playbook-for-crafting-ai-strategy/.

98. Cornell University. Copyright (C) 2024 Cornell University, https://www.cornell.edu/.

99. Boomi. "Cornell University Prepares Students for Job Market With Boomi in the Classroom." Boomi, April 3, 2023. https://boomi.com/blog/cornell-university-prepares-students-for-job-market-with-boomi-in-the-classroom/.

100. "Winners Dream: A Journey From Corner Store to Corner Office: McDermott, Bill, Gordon, Joanne, n.d., https://www.amazon.com/Winners-Dream-Journey-Corner-Office/dp/1476761086.

101. Buonfantino, Giusy. "Data Shows Shoppers Prioritizing Sustainability and Values." *Google Cloud Blog* (blog), April 27, 2022. https://cloud.google.com/blog/topics/consumer-packaged-goods/data-shows-shoppers-prioritizing-sustainability-and-values.

102. "Barbara Davis Center," n.d., https://medschool.cuanschutz.edu/barbara-davis-center-for-diabetes.

103. Erica Tulfo. "Brands should avoid this popular term. It's turning off customers," CNN.com, August 19, 2024, https://www.cnn.com/2024/08/10/business/brands-avoid-term-customers.

Index

Note: Page numbers in *italics* denote figures.

263

Index

Credit Union of Colorado, 131–136, 149

CRM (customer relationship management) system
   Australian Red Cross, 16
   automation, 110–111
   connectivity to other systems, 26, 83, 90
   selecting applications, 47

curiosity, 218

customer experience
   fragmented, 17
   generative AI through APIs, 139
   poor from disconnected systems, 54
   real-time data access, 91

customer relationship management. *see* CRM (customer relationship management) system

customer service
   AI-infused automation, 114–115
   support problems caused by fragmentation, 53

cybercrime, 62, 70

dark data, 80–81

data
   accessibility of, 34–35, 45, 97
   accuracy, 86–88, 92, 93, 114–115
   actionable, 84, 222
   big, 195
   checklist for preparing for AI, 92–93
   clean, 92
   connectivity, 85, 88–93
   consolidation, 92
   dark, 80–81
   disconnected, 75–76, 80, 82, 88
   Four Vs of data analytics, 81–82, 223
   fuel for AI engine, 35, 85
   governance, 92
   as heart of AI, 71
   integration and sharing methods, 55–57
   knowing your, 222
   as knowledge and power, 78
   liquidity, 84–85
   LLM training, 158
   manual updating of, 76
   moving, 88, 90, 93, 222
   as new oil, 82, 84
   as primary competitive advantage, 87
   proprietary, 8, 35, 85, 93, 114, 195, 210, 224–225, 231
   quality, 87, 92–93
   as sand, 82–85
   security, 92
   semi-structured, 83
   sources, number of, 24–25
   sprawl, 50, 83, 93
   storage, 90, 93
   strategic asset, 10
   structured, 83
   training models with, 85–87
   trust, 80–81, 86, 88, 115, 195, 226, 231
   unstructured, 83
   unsynchronized, 90
   useful, 84
   value, 81–82, 84–85, 88, 222, 223
   variety, 223
   velocity, 81, 223
   veracity, 81, 223
   visibility, 93
   volume, 81–85, 87, 223

data access, real-time, 91, 92
data centers, spending on, 31
data discovery, 163, 169
data entry, 83
data hub, 90, 91
DataHub, Boomi, 91, 105

267

Index

271

Index

Tropicana Brands Group (TBG),
151–156
truth, single source of, 90, 195, 215
truths, universal, 20–21
TurboTax, 117–118

Unbundling the Enterprise (McLarty
and Fishman), 84, 139
unified platform, 64, *189–190*, 191
unintended consequences, 22–25
universal truths, 20–21
University of Colorado Hospital,
239
use cases, low-hanging fruit,
220–221

value
  adding, 107
  business, 30, 35, 94, 143, 198,
    213, 227
  data, 81–82, 84–85, 88, 222

values, and brand alignment with
shoppers, 238
van de Keuken, Teun, 182
velocity, data, 81
vendors, partners of, 198
veracity, data, 81
Vianai Systems, 167, 171, 176
virtual assistant, 160–161
visibility, data, 93
visibility and control,
119–120
volume, data, 81–85, 87

Wang, R "Ray," 86, 114
Wilson, Brett, 16–20
Winners Dream (McDermott),
237
Workday, 234
Wynn Resorts, 126

Young Parents Program, 17

The world is a better place when we're all connected.

Now that Steve Lucas has shared his vision for an integrated, automated, and AI-ready business, meet the Boomi team that can make it happen – and can help you achieve outcomes that make a difference.

Visit Boomi.com for resources, including:

- Product Demos
- Blogs
- eBooks
- Podcasts
- Case Studies
- Webinars
- Free Trial

Boomi.com